5.95

CHRI
LEADE

DAVID SPRIGGS

p 82 118

AIRS/GRACES p 120-1

Delegation 123-129

Growth → new leadership roles p130ff

Quotes for BBCourse: p 130-1

esp. p160-1 Premises of leadership

BIBLE SOCIETY

CONTENTS

British and Foreign Bible Society
Stonehill Green, Westlea, Swindon, SN5 7DG, England

First published 1993

ISBN 0-564-08425-5

Cover Design by Jane Taylor
Printed and bound in Great Britain by Biddles Ltd, Guildford

PREVIEW

Thank you for opening this book.

I wonder why you are looking at it? Maybe you are in a bookshop and the cover attracted you. Perhaps you want to be a better leader in your situation, or maybe you are intrigued as to why your leaders act as they do, or you may wish to help and encourage your own leaders. Whatever the reason, I am pleased our lives have intersected. Naturally, I hope that you will want to stay longer; perhaps to flip through the rest of the book... best of all, to join with others in using the book to help one another grow into our leadership potential. Then you will be a more creative and helpful person in the Christian community and find more personal fulfilment too.

Even if you must now put the book down and our lives never touch again, I thank you. Why? For you have made my effort in writing it more worthwhile. If you can stay with me a few moments why not ask yourself these questions:

Why is he writing this way?

Is he succeeding?

If you want to know my view please turn to page 173.

FOREWORD

Working Together

It is my hope that together we, and others with whom you may share the experience of this book, will be able to move forward into being the kind of leaders God wants for today's Church. It is also my hope that God will be better able to use us to help his people move forward into his will. But first, a word about how this book came to be written.

I am very grateful to my church that they allowed me two six-week periods of study to investigate the theme of Christian leadership. The reasons for this were, first, that I knew I needed to improve my own leadership to play my part properly in a developing church situation. Secondly, I realized the importance of appropriate leadership and the need to train others for leadership in the church. I was aware that my own college equipped me by "absorption" rather than by addressing this issue specifically. I was faced with the issue of how best to use this time. I felt God telling me very clearly that the first phase should be spent visiting as many of the local Christian leaders as possible. In all I visited about sixty of them. Although this was an inner call it made sense to me, on reflection, as I was then chairman of the Coventry Council of Churches. But, of course, I shared this thought with leaders in my church and the Council of Churches who endorsed its value.

At that time I did not know where it would lead but I discovered three general attitudes:

1. Visionary — where the leader dreamed dreams for his church and sought to turn his dreams into plans.
2. Maintenance — where the leader saw his role as trying to sustain things as they were. Often this was not the result of apathy or laziness but basically because maintenance absorbed all his energies.
3. Retreating — not in the religious sense but the military one, where survival techniques were the most necessary skills, sometimes surviving against the congregation, the environment or even the building.

There is no criticism implied in these observations. Indeed I was impressed, and somewhat surprised, by the dedication and commitment of people in all three categories. But I was also stirred to believe that, with such commitment, energies could be directed in a more fruitful way for God's kingdom. I realized that resourcing the churches with more leadership was a key factor in doing this. Even Moses found that some redirection of talents and energies was needed, and that this need may have to be pointed out:

> *The next day Moses was settling disputes among the people, and he was kept busy from morning till night. When Jethro saw everything that Moses had to do, he asked, "What is all this that you are doing for the people? Why are you doing this all alone, with people standing here from morning till night to consult you?"*
>
> *Then Jethro said, "You are not doing it the right way." (Exodus 18.13, 14.17.)*

I expect Moses felt threatened to start with but he was wise enough to accept Jethro's advice and to realize what a difference it would make for himself and the people. So, I believe, it will do for our churches. Notice how the "must" of verse 15 can soon change.

1 Samuel 17 tells another story about the impact which leadership can make on a defeated situation. But my book is not about ousting the present leadership by brilliant solo performances. Rather, it is about developing a wider leadership base so that:

1. The main leader is relieved of as many commitments as is helpful.
2. Others can be involved in their God-appointed tasks in a proper way.
3. There is room for real growth, not in bureaucracy, but in personal maturity in Christ, both in numbers and in social effectiveness.

The groundwork for the book was developed in the second six weeks. Having sketched a plan I then felt led by God to leave it. This was not an easy thing for an organizer like myself to do, but in God's wonderful way, a few months later, completely unsought, the opportunity to write this book came along.

I am grateful for the chance to share this opportunity for growth in leadership with you, not least because it tells me God is managing a growing Church and you are to be part of his leadership team.

Task

Read Exodus 18.13–27 and see how many notable points about leadership and delegation you can see.

Imagine you were Jethro. How might you make his point to Moses? What were Jethro's feelings towards Moses and how might he have communicated them?

PREFACE

In writing this book I am aware that I need to hit two targets at once. An impossible aim unless you help me by lining up the targets! I realize that I will be addressing central leaders, often the sole paid full-time leader, such as vicars, ministers or full-time elders. People who will be wanting, for many reasons, to encourage and equip others for leadership among God's people.

I am also writing for members of the congregation, some of whom are already functioning as leaders and who want to help the central leader, maybe as Jethro helped Moses, maybe by being a more useful leader. Others will feel they do not hold any leadership post but are preparing themselves, however tentatively, for this possibility. Obviously the issues appear differently from different positions. It would be tedious to write the book from both perspectives so please help me by making the necessary adjustments throughout the book to suit your situation.

However, such an exercise is itself a very necessary part of our preparation for leadership at whatever level. We need to be as aware as possible of what it is like to be in the other person's place in order to carry out our responsibility adequately.

I find 1 Peter 5.1–4 an illuminating passage.

> *I, who am an elder myself, appeal to the church elders among you. I am a witness of Christ's sufferings, and I will share in the glory that will be revealed. I appeal to you to be shepherds of the flock that God gave you and to take care of it willingly, as God wants you to, and not unwillingly. Do your work, not for mere pay, but from a real desire to serve. Do not try to rule over those who have been put in your care, but be examples to the flock. And when the Chief Shepherd appears, you will receive the glorious crown which will never lose its brightness.*

In it the following structure appears:

Christ		Chief shepherd
Peter	Church elders	Shepherds
	Congregation	Flock

In fact, there is no clear distinction between shepherds and sheep.

The elders to whom Peter appeals (with due humility) are the sheep that Jesus committed to his care (John 21.17). The flock to which they, as elders, are to give an example are, in a way, also potential elders. (Shepherds don't give an example to sheep. Who wants sheep to walk on two legs and carry a crook!) The whole point is that every one of us is at the same time a leader and a follower (someone who is led), as even Peter was, for he had his chief shepherd, Jesus. We are also those people who are giving as well as receiving lessons in leadership. This is, of course, reinforced by Jesus' own teaching that he who is greatest must be the chief servant etc. So we are all learners, leaders, and led; and the effort to understand the other perspective is necessary for us whether we are an archbishop or a new convert. So our problem is, in fact, a great plus in helping us to be better at leading and following.

I also recognize that people will use this book in three main ways. Each will have its value and they are mutually compatible. Hopefully, one way will lead to another. Besides reading the book as any other book, which is useful for familiarization, we can use it in the following contexts:

Context 1. Use the book as a personal text book. This will include working through some of the tasks, even if, for many of them, it will only be imagining how things might work out.

Context 2. Use the book as a personal text book but involve **prayer partners.** Prayer partners are people you trust and sense love you, who commit themselves to pray for you and help you develop your leadership capability. Growing in Christian leadership is a spiritual matter and, therefore, benefits greatly from utilizing God's resources. At the end of the book is a draft letter (see page 175) you might send, or adapt, or use as a guide for your verbal request, to those you select as prayer partners. If you have prayer partners you are already becoming a leader even if you don't have any other leadership responsibility. Normally two prayer partners are adequate.

Context 3. Use this book as a group based exercise. The following is an example of the commitment required to maximize the value of this book using it this way. It is helpful for anyone leading such a group to share this commitment and obtain acceptance. This makes it easier to support each other.

Course Requirements

1. A God-given desire to be a better Christian leader or a better Christian follower.
2. A Bible and notebook.
3. Two prayer partners, willing to meet once a week.
4. A truthful and loving spouse or close friend.
5. Willingness to attend all the course (unless unavoidably prevented), of one and a half hours per week.
6. Willingness to work through at least one task per chapter/session (up to two hours per week).
7. Commitment to pray for the leader of the course and the other members of the course.
8. Willingness to change and be changed by God.
9. Willingness to talk things through and share with other course members (in small groups) and one to one with the leader (four times during the course).

Many of the tasks can be modified to work in any of the three contexts but the following signs indicate their primary context(s).

○ Context 1
△ Context 2
× Context 3

CHAPTER 1

WHY CHRISTIAN LEADERSHIP?

> *"Leadership ... the means by which authority is made effective"*[1]

Goal

To consider the significance of leadership for today's Church.

Aims

1. To consider the inevitability and importance of leadership in general.
2. To review reasons for the need for good Christian leadership in today's churches.
3. To understand what is meant by Christian leadership.
4. To become aware of the impact of secular leadership on our Christian views.
5. To alert us to the need for a critical stance to secular leadership.
6. To examine whether the drive for leadership is itself a secular influence by summarizing the place of leadership in the Bible.

Main Scriptures

Romans 12.1, 2; Psalm 119.9–16.

Why Bother with Leaders?

"I don't know what we pay them for!" We can imagine such a comment being made about M.P.s, the manager of a defeated soccer club, or even the Church's leaders. In moments of disappointment or frustration it is normal to blame the leaders. Do we really need leaders?

Leaders are usually expensive! They tend to expect or receive larger salaries or other financial advantages. But they also make demands on other people, expect to be obeyed and restrict other people's freedom. Sometimes they can cause enormous damage. Why do we have them and why do we put up with them? These are important questions to ask whether we are thinking about leaders in government, the military, trade unions, business, education or the family. They also apply to ecclesiastical leaders! Are leaders there because, either through ability or hierarchy, they have wheedled themselves into the positions of power, or are they there because for some reason or other they have a necessary role to play for the well being of the groups of people they lead? Perhaps a final answer to these questions cannot be given for any individual or type of leader. As Christians, however, we would say that unless the leaders make a valuable contribution to the group their *raison d'être* is extremely doubtful. So are leaders, or at least the leadership, inevitable?

Most of us have dreamed of a classless society. In his deceptively simple book, *Lord of the Flies*[2], William Golding portrays what happens when a group of apparently innocent choir boys suddenly find themselves released from those who control them. Through an aeroplane crash they find themselves set free on an uninhabited island. The island has sufficient resources not only for survival but for adventure, growth, development and, sad to say, destruction and death. Although the boys are free, soon leaders of different kinds start to come to the fore, and many degrees of oppression develop. In the end they are rescued, not accidentally I think, by the military!

William Golding is saying that leaders will emerge inevitably in any kind of group of human beings. Is he right? Why is leadership inevitable? Groups of people always have aims to accomplish. Often, of course, these aims are not stated, often they are not clarified or prioritized. The aims, maybe, conflict with each other, but nevertheless there are aims. Often a family, the group with which the majority of us are most familiar, has many aims, for example to help one another survive, to develop, to enjoy life. These grand aims are subdivided into more basic aims such as to protect ourselves from the weather by having a house, to have food to keep us alive, to love and care for one another and pass on information, to have a pleasant environment, such as the garden, in which to enjoy ourselves. The person who leads in each area may be different. Father may lead in terms of providing for and maintaining the house, mother in ensuring that food is available and the garden kept in order. Nevertheless, in most families leadership is being exercised; sometimes, of course, most effectively by the children who manipulate the parents with great skill! But unless the family is completely uncoordinated and chaotic, in which case it will not survive, leadership is being exercised.

So leadership helps the group to achieve its ends as effectively as possible. Leadership is not there to meet the ego needs of those who lead, although that is a constant danger which the group's members watch out for and seek to minimize. Leadership is essentially a servant function. That is why leadership is so important and also appropriate within Christian organizations. Churches and many other kinds of Christian groups have aims to achieve. Therefore leadership is important and, I think, inevitable. Because our main aims are so important leadership becomes even more crucial. Our aims are not ones which come from within the group, as those suggested for the family, they are aims which we receive from God, for example Genesis 1.28 "Have many children, so that your descendants will live all over the earth and bring it under their control." Deuteronomy 6.5 "Love the Lord your God with all your heart, with all your soul, and with all your strength." Matthew 28.19 "Go, then, to all peoples everywhere and make them my disciples..." Luke 10.9 "...heal the sick... and say... 'The Kingdom of God has come near you'."

Such aims are not primarily about the survival of the group members, but about the part God has given to us in his grand purpose of bringing all things in the universe into their proper relationship with each other, under the headship of Christ (Colossians 1.15–20). So we have the highest motivation to ensure that we have the best kind of leadership to help us all fulfil these aims, and if we are leaders of some kind, it is vital we are the best that we can be, not mainly for our own satisfaction, but to help God's people do God's work.

We can see there are many ways in which groups small and large, local, national and international, seek to organize themselves to achieve their aims. We can see that sometimes leaders help and sometimes hinder the progress of the group. So, whilst leadership is inevitable, we also soon learn that leadership is not automatically helpful. Again this spurs us on to want the best kind of leadership for God's people. Any survey of groups and leaders soon shows up that the group members have a vital part in proving and maintaining helpful leadership. So we are all involved in this process in the churches too.

Leadership is always important for God's people but there are crucial times in the development of groups. Times when the right leader can have a profound effect, but also times when the group has a vital part in helping the leaders to be right. I believe that leadership is a priority issue for all Christian people now.

The Churches Today

Here are some reasons why I consider leadership is a Christian priority:

1. There are new possibilities for growth. For instance, the number of people who have attended the Bible Society Church Growth course (1,298 during 1991–1992) indicates a desire for growth and a commitment to make it happen.
2. There are many changes in society, some brought about by government policy, some by changes in international politics and commerce, some by ecological change and awareness, some by changes in social patterns within our country, some by advances in technology, science, and medicine. The Church needs to respond to all of these. Such response needs leadership if it is to be as appropriate and effective as possible.
3. There is evidence that Christian people are willing to respond to strong and imaginative leadership. We can mention Billy Graham's Livelink, the Make Way marches, the development of Christian Aid, many of the house church arrangements, the situation in Northern Ireland with the Rev Ian Paisley etc, the part Christian leaders have played in Eastern Europe, and so on. Such responses will only benefit the kingdom of God if the leadership is right. So we are all involved in making sure that the leadership throughout the whole Christian body is as Christian as possible.
4. There are clearly many contentious issues about Christian leadership. For instance, the debate about women priests, the level of "shepherding", the proper structuring of the Christian churches internally and mutually. The number of books about these issues, and the vigour with which the discussions are carried out, indicate that leadership is a vital area of concern for Christians.
5. Perhaps the most immediately relevant reason is that there is a growing openness throughout the Christian denominations to

accept lay leadership. (Lay leadership — oh dear how we struggle for an adequate, inoffensive term! Some voluntary leaders can be ordained! Some paid Christian leaders are not! Some voluntary leaders have professional qualifications, some ordained paid leaders don't! When I use lay leadership I am using it fairly loosely to describe those people who have a supporting role, an auxiliary role to the official clergy. They may belong to para-church organizations, they may be volunteers, paid or unpaid etc. Those who fit this group vary from context to context so please help me by inserting your appropriate members for this difficult phrase!)

There are several contributory factors to this openness, such as a growing shortage of clerical leaders in some denominations, especially those which depend most heavily on ordained men for leadership, a recognition that the involvement of all God's people in the whole life of the Church is God's strategy, that there are many tasks to be done and much expertise needed to accomplish God's will in an increasingly complex world, and that less and less will ordained people alone be able to provide all that is needed. Such factors mean that developing our leadership (whether as an ordained person we read this as "developing those with ability to lead in our churches" or as a lay leader we read it to mean "developing my/our leadership abilities" or as a follower "helping our leaders to be better at their task") is a vital matter for us.

Of course we recognize that the (un)willingness of churches to accept and utilize lay leadership is a powerful limiting factor in the effectiveness of leadership but, even where Christian people are most resistant to this, I am sure we cannot avoid the challenge of providing the best leadership we can.

But such improvement in our ability to lead in a Christian way will have repercussions all round. Hopefully we shall make our secular leadership more Christian too. With this in mind it is worth briefly reviewing the different contexts in which people exercise leadership, or could do so. Perhaps it will help to note the specific ways in which you are involved.

We can lead:
at home:

at work:

in our community:

in our leisure activity:

other:

Imagine we are in a supermarket and come across a two year old in distress. If we are their parent we lead because of our role, if we are just there then it is accidental leading. How we handle the situation will be affected by the kind of Christian leadership we exercise. We can ignore them because we are busy, avoid them because we are frightened our involvement will be misunderstood, go and fetch the manager or do something to comfort them. We can easily think of everyday situations where leadership will affect the outcome.
Other situations:

This book aims to encourage the Christian leadership we provide in ordinary situations. For instance, with the double glazing salesman or talking to the home help. So even if we have no official position it will help us. But this book also invites us to help other Christians become as effective as possible in their Christian leadership and all of us can contribute to this.

Why Christian Leadership?

Why speak about Christian leadership and what is meant by it anyway? For Christian groups with Christian objectives the "best" situation involves having Christian leadership, not merely Christians who lead. We can consider various possibilities and it is worth asking which group we come into:

1. People can be Christian but not good, or not as good as they could be, at the process of leading.
2. People can be Christian but have not allowed their being Christian to have properly or fully affected and infiltrated their leading.
3. People can be leading in a Christian group but not in fact be Christian.

What we want is Christian people who have developed their leadership ability to its full potential and have allowed their being Christian to transform their leadership.

Romans12.1,2 is a very important passage.

So then, my brothers, because of God's great mercy to us I appeal to you: Offer yourselves as a living sacrifice to God, dedicated to his service and pleasing to him. This is the true worship that you should offer. Do not conform yourselves to the standards of this world, but let God transform you inwardly by a complete change of your mind. Then you will be able to know the will of God — what is good and is pleasing to him and is perfect.

There is a constant tendency for the secular environment to shape us (or rather deform us) and we need to counteract this by allowing Christian attitudes to penetrate our whole life style, including our leadership.

This does not mean we must reject all secular insights about leading. There are many examples of the positive difference that leaders can make. In politics I think particularly of Mr Gorbachov and the impact he made on Russian society. Coming from Coventry it is natural for me to think of the transformation that John Egan has made to Jaguar cars. Anyone watching an interactive game like football, hockey or rugby knows the difference a good referee can make to the fulfilment of players and the enjoyment of spectators. Rather than rejecting secular insights we need to claim them for Christ.

Even if we are oblivious to them secular attitudes influence us. So, rather than absorb them naively, we need to be alert to the processes. For instance, we can recognize that secular leadership ideals affect us by the way our parents nurtured us, through the education we get, by absorbing society's attitudes and values and, increasingly, by the specific job related training which people receive. We need to evaluate these factors from our Christian perspectives.

Inevitably we must face the task of selecting what is the best way for Christians to lead. Here the Christian community has a varied but vital role to play in helping to filter out those processes of leading which are inappropriate for Christian leaders. That is one reason why it is helpful to use this book in a group context and to have prayer partners. This is why many of the tasks are best done with other Christians. But this process can, and should, go on continuously by involving people in our groups to help us check our leadership and, if we are followers, checking those who lead.

Another vital stage in this process is exposing ourselves mentally, emotionally and spiritually to the Bible. Psalm 119 probably had its home among those who had a leadership role in Israel. Its words are instructive.

How can a young man keep his life pure?
By obeying your commands.
With all my heart I try to serve you...
I keep your law in my heart...
I study your instructions...
I take pleasure in your laws; (Psalm 119.9–16 part).

If we want to keep our leadership continually transformed we need constantly to surrender it to the insight of Scripture, highlighted by the Holy Spirit. Throughout this book we shall be seeking to do this, and the next chapter concentrates on this.

Is Leadership a Christian Concern?

Before we move into this process there is a fundamental question we should ask. Clearly there are many books about Christian leadership appearing at the moment. Is this merely a reflection of secular obsession with leadership or is it a proper Christian concern? It is not enough to establish there are reasons for it, we have to be sure they are Christian reasons. Expediency is not enough.

As soon as we turn to Scripture it seems to me we are brought face to face with the significance of leaders and leadership for God's people. Positively we think of Moses, David, Nehemiah, Jesus, Peter, Paul etc. Negatively we think of Adam, Saul, Rehoboam, Judas etc.[3]

The problems of the time of the judges are summarized in the words "There was no king in Israel at that time. Everyone did just as he pleased." (Judges 21.25, and Judges 17.6). In other words there was no God appointed leadership and the results were disastrous. It is well known that there appear to be two different evaluations of the monarchy in the Bible (e.g. 1 Samuel 10.1–16, 17–7) but essentially the divergence is not about the need for leadership but about the difficulty of keeping it God centred (Deuteronomy 17.14–20).

Although the book of Revelation tells us there is no temple, or even sun, in heaven because they are unnecessary there is a very real sense of leadership being exercised in the orderliness of heaven and the central focus of him who sits on the throne and the lamb.

Scripture throughout bears witness to the vital role of leaders among God's people, but also emphasizes the dangers and difficulties of maintaining its fully Christian nature. Hence our task is, in the light of Scripture, a most important one.

Yet there is still one issue we need to consider. This book is about developing leaders, and about training them to be more effective. In the light of Scripture is this right? Is it not for God to call and equip? Are not the gifts which God gives through his Holy Spirit sufficient?

Sometimes people distinguish between two kinds of leaders. First, institutional leaders like priests and kings (in the New Testament perhaps like bishops and elders) and secondly charismatic leaders like judges and prophets (in the New Testament perhaps like apostles and evangelists).[4] Both types have a place in God's strategy but I believe both benefit from training. Leaders are neither only born, nor even born of the Spirit. Essential as these factors are they also need to be developed. Our personality and nurture can contribute to our effectiveness as Christian leaders. Our spiritual birth and gifting from the Holy Spirit are, I would maintain, prerequisites for any level of Christian leadership. Nevertheless these natural and supernatural basics can be enhanced by training. It is clear throughout the Bible that God arranged for the training of his leaders. For instance, Moses through his upbringing in Pharaoh's court, as well as his period as a shepherd under Jethro. The disciples are trained by Jesus, Paul is always looking for people to train and encouraging his leaders to do the same (e.g. 1 Timothy 4.6–15; 2 Timothy 2.2).

But right methods are never enough, hence we shall encourage the use of all God's resources for this process of developing our leadership, including the resources of prayer and fellowship, the Scriptures and the Holy Spirit. Hence, too, we shall be emphasizing growth in Christlikeness of character as well as performance. Nevertheless, we cannot avoid the aim of Christian leadership. This is to provide the leadership which will help Christian groups achieve their God given tasks. As Paul said of the ascended Christ:

> *It was he who "gave gifts to mankind"; he appointed some to be apostles, others to be prophets, others to be evangelists, others to be pastors and teachers. He did this to prepare all God's people for the work of Christian service, in order to build up the body of Christ. (Ephesians 4.11–12)*

Effective Christian leaders will contribute to the growth of God's Church numerically and qualitatively. This will glorify God and that is our chief end. Effective Christian leadership is a high priority for all Christian people.

So to give time to working with, and through, this book will help to build the kingdom of God and will enhance the fulfilment of our living as people and our witness as Christians in all areas of our lives.

Tasks

At the end of each chapter there are, as here, a variety of growth exercises. Some are best done individually, some require working on with others. Sometimes they have been mentioned as relevant at some point in the text. It would be well nigh impossible to do them all at once but to benefit from this book it is important to do one or more for each chapter. There are many different styles of exercise. To start with do some which seem easy and comfortable to you but eventually try to work at those which seem more alien. Often these, in the end, surprise us by being more enjoyable than we imagined and certainly more beneficial than we could guess. If you start on one and it doesn't go well, leave it and try again later as you work through the book again.

For many of us number 5 is a comfortable place to start — although the analysis might not be quite so comforting! If, as I hope you can, you are meeting with prayer partners please be sure to look at number 7.

If you are the leader of a group using this book it is possible to start by using some of the training exercises and to feed in the issues of the text in evaluating the exercises. This may be the best way for groups which find activities the best way for learning.

Please adapt the ideas to suit your situation or context. As a reminder, the following symbols are used:

○ — on your own
△ — with prayer partner
× — in a group

○ × 1. Obtain or compile a list of leaders in your church. Select six different levels and kinds of leadership. Establish clearly their responsibilities. What age, occupation and experience do they have? How, if at all, does their Christian leadership relate to their secular leadership? Do they lead at the same level, do they have responsibilities for similar issues in both, do they require different, or the same, skills and attitudes?

○ × 2. Interview two leaders in your church to discover what their jobs are, how they carry them out and what help they have and need. First, decide who you will select. Then, think about how to make the approach:

What do they need to know?
How can you best communicate it?
What options do you have?
What sort of questions do you need to ask them?

After you have interviewed them consider what you have learnt about how people lead and how to relate positively to leaders.

○ 3. List different kinds of leadership you experience or exercise in church, work, home, community, or leisure. Consider and note down how you respond in these situations and what affects your response. If it is difficult to do this retrospectively keep a note for a week.

○ × 4. Record leadership situations you are involved in this week (or lack of leadership!). Why did the leaders act as they did? Work out different approaches and whether they would help or hinder.

○ × 5. Watch your favourite TV programmes. (Who said books were boring!) Better still, video two or three of them. Consider how Christian the leadership styles are that you have been absorbing. How might you, as a Christian person, have handled the situations differently? How does your normal attitude to these TV programmes reflect your Christian commitment?

○ × 6. Write a short sketch about an irate customer at a supermarket checkout. The operator calls the supervisor who tries to pacify the customer. Meanwhile the other customers in the queue are getting restless.
Either in a group play out the various roles and explore your feelings and responses, or individually consider other ways your sketch could have turned out.
How might different leadership from the customer, operator, and supervisor have affected the situations? What difference would good Christian leadership have made in each role?

△ 7. Please arrange your first meeting with your prayer partners and explain why you need them to pray for you, that you would like to meet at least once between each session (fix some dates, times and venues) and that you would like them to ask you questions, for example
What have you learnt?
What challenged you most?
What are you finding most difficult?
What would you like them to pray for most?
Ensure they know you are willing to pray for them also for specific things. A very important part of our growth into leadership will be growth in our experience of prayer.

References — Chapter 1

1. Peter Nott "Towards a Theology of Leadership", *Expository Times,* February, 1986, p.138.
2. William Golding, *Lord of the Flies* (Faber, 1954).
3. For a brief discussion of this issue see B W Anderson, *The Living World of the Old Testament,* (Longmans, 1958), pp.116–121.
4. For a survey of the Old Testament issues see W Ecchrodt, *Theology of the Old Testament I* (SCM,1961) pp. 289–456.

CHAPTER 2

WHAT MAKES LEADERSHIP CHRISTIAN?

"Christian leadership, in contrast to secular leadership, is based on servanthood. There is no other way to get it".[1]

Goal

To understand the nature of Christian leadership and how the Bible can help our leadership to be more Christian.

Aims

1. To explore the nature of Christian leadership by considering a story and a situation.
2. To consider three New Testament models of leadership.
3. To help assimilate the insights of these models into our lives.
4. To indicate other ways of absorbing appropriate biblical material.

Main Scriptures

John 13.1–16; Luke 12.42–48; 1 Peter 4.7–11; John 10.1–16

In the first chapter I promised that in this chapter we would concentrate on using the insights of Scripture to ensure that our leadership is continually becoming more Christian. But first we must examine more carefully what we mean by Christian leadership. Jesus told the parable of the Good Samaritan to illustrate what being a good neighbour meant. In so doing, with his penetrating humour, he revealed several anomalies in the way people normally think about "being good". Being good is not the same as being Jewish, or keeping yourself pure to carry out religious ceremonies in the temple etc. Being good can mean you belong to the wrong race (Samaritan) and you are going in the wrong direction (from

Jerusalem instead of to it), as long as you are willing to risk your life and to pay any price to help someone in need. We can look at a similar story to help us consider some of the issues about being a good Christian leader.

Scene One: Late Saturday Night

After attending a musical performance at Coventry Cathedral Graham Spencer, a pleasant, well-dressed man of thirty, made his way towards the railway station to catch his train back to Birmingham. He was carrying his briefcase and an umbrella. The briefcase contained, among other things, the musical scores for the concert. As he walked under one of the underpasses he was mugged. His clothes were torn, his briefcase snatched, his wallet taken and he was dragged, half dead, and dumped in the public gardens nearby, known as Greyfriars Green.

Scene Two: Sunday Morning at 9.00 am

At 9.00 am prompt on Sunday morning as Mrs Jones, the director of the church choir, walked to worship she saw Graham who, by now, looked dishevelled and unkempt, lying in the bushes. She thought to herself,"What a shame! How sad that people waste their bodies on drink and end up like this". She hurried on, her mind full of divine thoughts and the anthem the choir would soon sing to the glory of God under her direction.

A few minutes later Will Latham, the newly appointed chief steward for the city centre Baptist Church, hurried across Greyfriars Green. He caught sight of the body slumped in the bushes and went over to examine it. He was half tempted to investigate further but when he thought of all that needed doing at church to prepare for worship he knew he didn't have time, so he hurried on. So many people were depending on him, he had to fulfil his Christian responsibilities. It was all the more important as he wanted to impress people, particularly the previous chief steward, with his reliability.

Chas was a bit of a lad. He'd had a wonderful Saturday night with his crowd, and his girlfriend afterwards. The sun had woken him so he decided to go home for breakfast at 10.00 am. On his way he saw Graham's body. "Poor bloke", he said. He went over to him, dried him on his jacket, put his sweater over him and phoned his dad to bring the car. Together they took Graham to casualty (the ambulance drivers were on strike). They saw Graham all through the procedures in the hospital and into a bed. They promised to visit him every day. They left a £10 note on his locker and told the staff nurse to get him anything he needed.

Christian Leadership

Which of these was exercising Christian leadership? Of course, such a story is in many ways unfair, just as the story Jesus told was unfair. So if you feel the question is unfair you are probably right. Most directors of church choirs would, in practice, look at the person. If they were trained in first aid they would probably do something to help the injured person and, if not, at least they would find a public phone and report the situation to the police etc. However, our concern is not with the unfairness in the story but to use it to raise issues about Christian leadership.

In one sense both Mrs Jones and Will Latham were exercising Christian leadership. Both had been appointed to a task, they knew they had a job to do for the church and they were committed to doing it. We won't get far as leaders if we allow ourselves to be deflected by any and every need which crosses our path. In conducting the choir or enabling 400 people to worship because books and leaflets were given out properly, and the front of the church set out appropriately with the furniture in the required places and the microphones adjusted correctly, Mrs Jones and Will were being Christian leaders.

Where they went wrong was (we probably think) in not sorting out their priorities properly. A person's life or death situation was more *urgent* than their *important* responsibilities. In Mrs Jones' case her wrong course of action was compounded by her evaluation of the situation that he was just another unfortunate drunk (but doesn't everyone count because they are loved by God — but if it's their own fault should we take as much trouble — but then is it their own fault entirely — even if God loves them don't we need to take some account of the effectiveness of the energy and other resources we put into the situation). In Will's case his mistake was compounded because of his desire to impress people as he had only recently taken on the task. He was unsure of himself. He didn't have the mental freedom to cope with the unexpected because all his mind was concentrating on the many details he had to cover in the church.

We could argue that Mrs Jones' hasty moral condemnation, and Will's over-preoccupation with his own self esteem, suggest they were not suitable for such Christian leadership as they had. Most of us, I think, will do well not to argue this way. I don't find it hard to envisage situations in which I make wrong evaluations, or where my concern with my responsibility leads me to overlook an urgent and pressing opportunity for exercising Christian leadership. Indeed, one point of this parable is to raise the question as to whether being a Christian, let alone a perfect one, is necessary for our leadership to be Christian!

Chas (bless him!) makes no pretence at being a Christian, or probably a leader. It was relatively easy for him to help Graham Spencer. He had no other commitments, no people urgently dependent on him, he had no image to maintain and he had no tendency to condemn people for being drunk; he had been in that state himself a few times and didn't suffer from a non-conformist conscience!

The reason we can feel sympathy with Chas' course of action is that he did the caring, human thing instinctively. He is clearly generous hearted. He hadn't learnt to steward his resources carefully. He would spend his money when he had it, and if he hadn't any he would borrow off his mates or go without. He knew his dad would help anyone. So the whole operation was easy and natural for him.

What makes Leadership Christian?

One consideration is the nature of the *task* for which the leader is responsible. Singing to the glory of God, and helping others to worship God through that singing, are Christian tasks. Those who lead people to do such things are normally going to be exercising *Christian* leadership. However, it is not hard to envisage Dylan Thomas presenting us with a Mrs Jones who seems to do anything but exercise Christian leadership. In fact such a person would not really help the choir sing to the glory of God, but their own glory or her own glory. So the task does not guarantee that the leadership will be Christian. Because the task is overtly Christian it becomes even more imperative that the leadership is exercised by a Christian out of his or her Christian character.

However, church choirs and stewarding suggest another danger for us. It is easy to identify Christian with religious acts or church based functions. Not everything that goes on in churches is distinctively Christian. Not everything that goes under the name of religion is Christian, and certainly not everything that requires Christian leadership can be confined to such narrow limits. There is clearly the need for Christian leadership in the home, education, commerce, politics, industry, the arts, technology etc. We can imagine much of it being done better by non-Christians, although our mental comparisons will probably be "unfair", like Jesus' parable. So a second point to note is that the person exercising the leadership makes a crucial contribution as to whether or not the leadership is Christian. Chas got things right by chance, Christians should get them right out of their Christian character, training, and insight from the Holy Spirit.

A third factor is the *outcome.* Graham was helped when in great need. His health and dignity were restored, his confidence in human nature repaired by Chas and his father. When Christian outcomes take place Christians can rejoice. There was also something appealing about Chas' style of leadership. It was person centred. He involved others whom he knew were willing. It was supportive and non-condemnatory. Whether Chas would be good at taking difficult decisions we don't know, but often Christian insight, courage and integrity are vital then. Different situations will require different leadership styles if they are going to be as Christian as possible.

What about motives? Again Chas appeals to us because he didn't seem to have any ulterior motives, so we assume his motives were good, if not Christian. There are hints that for Mrs Jones and Will their motives contained some questionable elements. Would Chas' action have been more Christian if he had been doing it to serve Christ?

Considering a story, then, can help us see that determining what makes leadership Christian is not simple. Christians can exercise Christian leadership doing secular tasks. Non-Christians can act in a Christian way. Christians can be motivated by non-Christian motives and so on. What is clear is that all these aspects of our leadership need to be considered if we are going to make our leadership as Christian as possible. But how can we begin to allow Christ to transform our leadership?

In the Bible there are many kinds of material to help us but in some ways the most helpful is what I call "biblical models". Models are not personality or character studies. These can be restrictive because of their historical localization. Neither are models commands or exhortations, important as these may be for giving us general guidance about our leadership. Rather, models are pictures or images which, like the parables, have a certain timeless quality and great flexibility of application. They also have the advantage that they tend to cover several of the facets of Christian leadership we highlighted earlier. Out of the many biblical models of leadership I have chosen three: the servant, the steward, and the shepherd.

There are several reasons for this selection. First Jesus said, "As the Father sent me, so I send you" John 20.21. Jesus spoke these words to his leaders, so all Christian leadership should be modelled on Jesus. These are models which Jesus either claimed he fulfilled or did fulfil.

Secondly, there is something of a consensus among contemporary books on Christian leadership that these are important and central. Peter Nott writes,

> *It is impossible to construct a systematic doctrine of leadership adequate for today's purposes from the Old Testament and New Testament alone. But the sources for an understanding of Christian leadership are there and from them it may be possible to indicate styles and methods which are both true to Christian origins, though enlightened by more contemporary studies, and related to present needs.*[2]

He selects shepherd, servant, father, and body. John Finney, Philip King, and Philip Greenslade all choose servant, shepherd, and steward.[3]

Thirdly, there are many references to these models throughout Scripture. So as we read or listen to the Bible we are likely to have our understanding of them refreshed and filled out. This frequent jogging of our minds can be a reminder to check our progress in the process of transforming our leadership.

In order to make our learning from Scripture as helpful as possible we shall use three different methods as we explore the three different models.

The Servant (using the FIER method)

Many people, quite rightly in my opinion, see this as the essential model. The converse confirms this.

> *There is one title used in the New Testament to describe leadership that is* never *used of the Christian minister. There are 109 occurrences of the words which stem from* archon, *"a ruler"...used several times as a description of Christ himself; but never are they used to describe a Christian leader.* [4] *(see also Mark 10.42, 1 Peter 5.3)*

So the first model we need to take to heart is that of the servant. I use the phrase deliberately. Jesus himself realized its importance and also how difficult it is for us to grasp. In order to be servants we need to experience him serving us. Hence, for this model, I choose deliberately the FIER approach. This approach encourages us to experience the essential message of the passage, not only understand it. It helps us assimilate the truth of Scripture into our personal lives and reshape them on the basis of what we experience. The passage we will use is John 13.1–17. How do we proceed? If you are using this book as a group it is helpful that one of the group leads/serves the rest by taking you through the process. If not it is quite possible and effective to do it by yourself. I shall write for a group situation but it is easy enough to adapt for the individual. In any case if you are the leader of a group it is necessary to work through it first yourself.

Preparation (for the group leader)

A week or so before read through John 13.1–17 a few times. It can often help to use different translations. The reason for this is to familiarize yourself with the passage so that you can easily picture it yourself. Through a variety of translations different details or nuances will come to light. These will give a sense of freshness to what is a well-known story anyway and give you some awareness of the different ways people will hear the passage. There may also be a few details which you want to check out in the commentaries. Further, it is helpful to know the context of the passage, e.g. what precedes and what follows it. In the case of John's Gospel this also means the theological context of his gospel. Then, with paper and pen available, we are ready to proceed.

Introduction (to share with the group)

The purpose of this approach is to allow the Holy Spirit to use our imaginative and emotive faculties to help us experience the presence of Jesus through Scripture. Jesus promised that if we gather in his name he would be with us. He also told us that it is part of the work of the Holy Spirit to bring Christ's truth to us (John 14.25, 26; 15.26; 16.14). So first, having explained the purpose of this approach, we need to pray, claiming the promise of Jesus, because we meet in his name and asking the Holy Spirit to come to us to show us deeply the truth that Jesus was teaching. It is normally helpful to offer our whole selves to God (Romans 12.1, 2), especially our minds and imaginations.

Familiarization

First we can explain the context, then we give people five to ten minutes to read through the passage. We indicate that we want everyone to be at ease with the passage. So after an initial quiet, personal reading we ask them to close their eyes while we read the passage to them. It is important not to read too quickly so that people have time to start to picture the process recorded for us.

Identification

The next stage is to identify with someone in the passage. Our aim is not to be someone we fancy, but to allow God to show us with whom he wants us to identify. Only three people are specifically named in this passage — Jesus, Judas, and Simon Peter. However others are present. We know the names, and to some extent the personalities, of the other disciples. But there were possibly other people around who are not specified. Servants, for instance, would probably not be far away. Some people will know who God wants them to be, most will not. I have found the following approach helps people with identification. First we need to take the pressure off. We don't have to have a blinding light experience. Next, encourage people to picture the scene and evaluate from what kind of perspective they are viewing things. Is it through the eyes of Jesus? Are they the one who objects to what Jesus is doing? Are they one of the other disciples waiting for Jesus to come around, or is it more as an outside observer? Perhaps through noting their position as they imagine the scene they can ascertain who, or at least what kind of person, they are. If after ten minutes people have still not identified themselves then I encourage them to choose who they would like to be. God can be at work just as much in this conscious choice I have found!

Experience

Normally it is good to lead the group in another prayer at this point, asking God, through his Holy Spirit, to reveal himself to us, especially to bring the truth of this passage for us right into the centre of our lives. If the group is not used to a meditative approach probably fifteen to twenty minutes will seem long enough to them. Other groups might be comfortable with a longer period. Explain that we are going to allow our imaginations to free wheel through this passage, but the story is the rails that guide the wheels. People may go off at apparent tangents if that is what God chooses. So encourage them to be relaxed and to enter into the passage.

What happens for them through the story?
What was it like to see Jesus take the bowl and the towel?
Did they expect him to ask them to do the foot washing?
What was it like waiting for him to come to wash their feet?
Did they watch whilst he washed their neighbour's feet or did they avert their eyes?
Were they angry that Peter made such a fuss?
Did they understand what Jesus meant?
Did Jesus speak quietly to each disciple as he washed their feet?
What was it like when he washed yours?
How did he hold them?
How did the feet feel before, and during, and after?
What did he say to you?
Did you mind waiting after your turn whilst he washed the others?
What went through your mind as you waited?
What did his words about an example say to you?
What do they say to you?

We can stimulate people's imaginations with questions like these. They will then think of many other questions.

Some people will find this approach much easier than others. Do assure people that they don't have to achieve anything. It is time for God to work. If he doesn't say anything now he will probably use it later. My own experience is that often nothing happens for me until the point when I stop expecting it to!

It is helpful for people to jot down a few points to help them remember what has gone on and any insights they have gained. Some can do this throughout the process, others would find it disruptive. So two or three minutes before the end of this stage mention we will soon be finishing and encourage people to write things down, if they have not already done so.

An alternative approach with some groups would be to actually go through the foot washing experience. Someone might volunteer to be Jesus, or someone could be appointed. The group might, or might not, want to have its own Peter and Judas. Out of this experience too insights about servant leadership could be shared.

The review process which follows can be adapted for this even more realistic situation.

Review

Before moving to this phase we pray that the Holy Spirit will make clear to us the significance of our experiences. There are all kinds of ways this can be facilitated. Individuals can write an account of their experience, highlighting the points which seem important to them and then ask "What is this/these telling me?" Or in small groups people can relate their experiences and others can then be involved in commenting on the significance of the experience. Alternatively we can work with the whole group, first asking people with whom they identified, then prompting some to relate their experience. In this way all can benefit from, and gain insight into, the nature of servant leadership through the experience of a few. This is itself an experience of servant leading! The willingness to be vulnerable to help others is at the heart of this kind of leading. The support and respect which this may well generate for those who take these risks will itself be a valuable lesson.

It is important that the members of the group, in some way, work out the implications and applications of their experience for their own leadership. Then they can seek to involve their prayer partners in this growth process too.

The steward (using the Swedish method)

Why this model is as popular as the other two is not immediately clear. Jesus does not appear to have used it of himself, although his claim to only do what the Father tells him approaches it. Neither does it seem to have been used to describe Jesus. Indeed, in Hebrews a contrast is drawn between Jesus and Moses who was a steward in charge of God's household, but at least there are links with Jesus and this model (Hebrews 3.1–6). There are also strong links between stewarding and serving (cf. Luke 16.2–3; 1 Corinthians 4.1–2 — not the *Good News Bible*).

One reason for its popularity may be reflected in the *Good News Bible* translation "manager" (see Luke 16.2–3; Luke 12.42; 1 Peter 4.7–10), although there is no consistency in translation here (see 1 Corinthians 4.1–2; Titus 1.7). Ours is an age which has given great significance to managers and the process of managing. It also seems to reflect well the normal position of those who lead in the Church. We are not to understand ourselves as creating and/or running our own business. We are accountable to God, we are here to fulfil his plans yet we are giving freedom and dignity in the process.

To say this, however, is to run ahead of our own exposure to this biblical model. We shall look at two passages using the Swedish method. With this method we read through the passage and mark it using symbols to highlight certain issues e.g.

☼ things I have learnt
? things I don't understand
! things which involve change for me

For each passage I have written a few comments. Please take time to read, mark and, where possible, share your thoughts on each passage.

Luke 12.42–48

To become the steward, or the person running the household, is itself the reward for faithful service. To be a steward is clearly a privilege, but not one which gives relief from responsibility, rather it increases it. To be in charge of the household means we must act responsibly towards the master, to whom we are accountable.

It means we are also to take care of the other servants. We have to give them "their share of the food at the proper time". In all probability we shall have to resist pressure from the other servants to misbehave in the absence of the master. We shall have to keep them working at their tasks. However, we must not mistreat them or take advantage of them because they are not our servants. The absence of the master presents the steward with many temptations so we must constantly live with an acute awareness of the imminence of his return.

Being a steward means the master has shared his plan with us, and made clear what he wants to happen. Therefore failure to fulfil the master's plan, or blatant disregard of it, warrants severe punishment. These points seem to encapsulate many of the dynamics of Christian leadership so we can see why it is such a popular model for us today. We should also remember that the master speaks well of those who are faithful in the discharge of their duties (cf. Luke 19.11–17).

What have we learnt?
What don't we understand?
What do we need to do?

1 Peter 4.7–11

This is the second passage on being a steward which we shall look at.

We notice first the motivation of the end time with which this passage begins. "The end of all things is near" (verse 7). Secondly the stress on the qualities we need to pray for. We need to pray to know the master's plan. Thirdly, it is interesting to observe the attention given to caring for the other servants (verses 8–9). Fourthly, we recognize that God has entrusted us with gifts to use for him and for each other's good. They are not for our own satisfaction, or to draw attention to ourselves, or to enable us to feel superior or dominate others. However, we do need to be aware of the special gifts he has given to us. How else can we use them appropriately?

> What have we learnt?
> What don't we understand?
> What do we need to do?

If we have time we can fill out and confirm the insight we have gained so far by looking at further steward passages e.g. Matthew 24.45–51; 25.14–30; Luke 19.4–27.

The Shepherd: John 10.1–16 (using the question method)

Although most of us are urban people there is still valuable insight in the picture of the leader as a shepherd. Philip King says it is "One of the favourite Bible words used to describe the Christian leader". Jesus claims this title for himself and P Greenslade says "Of all the pictures of Jesus given in the gospels, the one which shows him as the Shepherd has a particular appeal and special relevance". John Perry even claims that here is "the perfect pattern for Christian leadership".[5]

It has a thoroughly biblical pedigree. God is the shepherd (Isaiah 40; Psalm 23). The leaders of Israel should be shepherds (Ezekiel 34) and so should the leaders of God's new people (1 Peter 5.4). It is well known that the title pastor means shepherd, but it is perhaps less clear to us that biblically the shepherd is a much stronger kind of leader than most of us picture with our romantic imaginations, and a much more practical, rugged responsibility than patting sheep on their heads! The passage from John's Gospel makes some of this clear for us.

Jesus said, "I am telling you the truth: the man who does not enter the sheepfold by the gate, but climbs in some other way, is a thief and a robber. The man who goes in through the gate is the shepherd of the sheep. The gatekeeper opens the gate for him; the sheep hear his voice as he calls his own sheep by name, and he leads them out. When he has brought them out, he goes ahead of them, and the sheep follow him, because they know his voice. They will not follow someone else; instead, they will run away from such a person, because they do not know his voice."

Jesus told them this parable, but they did not understand what he meant.

So Jesus said again, "I am telling you the truth: I am the gate for the sheep. All others who came before me are thieves and robbers, but the sheep did not listen to them. I am the gate. Whoever comes in by me will be saved; he will come in and go out and find pasture. The thief comes only in order to steal, kill, and destroy. I have come in order that you might have life — life in all its fullness.

"I am the good shepherd, who is willing to die for the sheep. When the hired man, who is not a shepherd and does not own the sheep, sees a wolf coming, he leaves the sheep and runs away; so the wolf snatches the sheep and scatters them. The hired man runs away because he is only a hired man and does not care about the sheep. I am the good shepherd. As the Father knows me and I know the Father, in the same way I know my sheep and they know me. And I am willing to die for them. There are other sheep which belong to me that are not in this sheepfold. I must bring them, too; they will listen to my voice, and they will become one flock with one shepherd." (John 10.1–16)

From this we can construct table 1 to help us grasp the main points. More details can be found in the many commentaries that are available.

On the basis of this brief analysis we can allow the passage to question our leadership. What follows is only one way. I hope that you will let this model guide and challenge your leadership or views about leadership by putting questions to you.

TABLE 1

Reference	Main subject	Real shepherd	Alternatives
Verses1–2	Entrance	Goes in through gate Recognized	Does not use gate Climbs over wall Is thief or robber
Verses 3–6	Relationship to sheep	Calls own sheep by name Recognized by own sheep Leads them out Followed by sheep	Don't know voice Sheep won't follow Sheep run away because frightened
Verses 12–13	Cost to shepherd	Willing to die for sheep because they belong to him	Hired man runs away at danger Does not really care
Verses 10,11,16	Functions of shepherd	Leads in and out to pasture Precedes them Protects from danger Gathers other sheep into one fold	Thief — to steal, kill, destroy Wolf snatches and scatters
Verse 9	Gate for sheep	Protects even at night time Provides entrance and exit in safety	

Can I be called a good shepherd or do some of the alternatives better describe me?

1. Am I a hired man? i.e. Am I doing this job for what I can get out of it? It isn't wrong to receive rewards for our Christian service (e.g. 1 Timothy 5.17) but it is wrong to do it only for the rewards. So how can I check? Am I as caring and encouraging towards those who don't praise me, approve of me or pay me? Alternatively, do I give more attention to those who shout loudest or who would complain most if I didn't?
2. Am I a thief or a robber? i.e. Am I stealing something which doesn't belong to me? Am I wanting to "own" people who are in my charge? Do I always fully recognize that they are God's sheep not mine? Do I try, in any way, to get them to do what I want and to do it my way? Or am I committed to helping them discover what God wants and enabling them to do that?
3. Am I a wolf? i.e. do I frighten people because of a desire to satisfy my own appetites and ego needs? For instance, am I absorbing them into my life, am I using their resources for my own ends, do they feel I am taking them over? Do I frighten people because of my strength, or because I am negative and fearful? Do I scatter them by being divisive or impatient or by gossiping?
4. Or am I in some ways like the good shepherd? What ways are these?

What is my relationship with the sheep?

1. "He calls his own sheep by name". Who are my sheep? How well do I know them? What are their favourite foods, TV programmes etc? Do I know what problems they have, or what worries them most? Do I know what changes they would like in their working life, their family, their Christian life? At what level of intimacy is my conversation with them? Is it only "Good morning, how are you?" or can we honestly share our feelings without fear?
2. "The sheep recognize his voice". How much of myself am I willing to share? Do I consider my life my own, or is it available to them? If I feel I need to protect myself or hide myself from the sheep why is that? Is it really a matter of my shy personality? Or is it that there are parts of my life I wouldn't want them to see? Am I like Jesus who chose the twelve "to be with him"?

The cost to the shepherd

Am I really willing to lay down my life for the sheep? What risks have I taken to help them in the last two years? What dangers have I encountered? What price am I paying for the privilege of leading (cf. 2 Corinthians 11.1–32)? Have I accepted criticism on their behalf? Have I defended them from sheep stealers (or was it a form of self-preservation?)

Functions of the shepherd

The shepherd leads the sheep out to feed them. Do I want the sheep to be healthy and fully developed, or do I secretly want to keep them stunted and undernourished so I remain superior and they continue to be dependent on me? Do I know what kind of food is right and where to find it for them? Even in dry seasons? How much trouble will I take to provide their pasture — study, personal care etc. Do I go ahead of the sheep to investigate issues and opportunities? Do I ensure that the grass is clear of dangers? Do I have the necessary vision to perceive the next step(s) and do I have a good sense of direction? How can I develop so as to be a better shepherd for those in my care? Am I open enough to welcome the other sheep that God brings?

Being the gate keeper too? (verse 3)

Who is the gate keeper here? Is it God, just as Jesus was the vine and his Father the gardener? Does this mean that the shepherd is authorized and recognized by those in charge? Do I have a good relationship with those who have a wider responsibility than I do?

The gate of the sheepfold (verses 7–10).

The shepherd lay down at night to block the entrance. Am I always available? How could this apply to my sheep? Do I pray without ceasing?

In the light of this one passage we can see that many thrusting challenges come to our own leadership. We need to remember three other things:

1. We are sheep too. Do we know our master's voice and are we following him?
2. We have to give account of our shepherding (1 Peter 5:7).
3. Some of us need to become ranchers rather than shepherds. This term is used by C P Wagner to indicate that with larger numbers of people to care for we cannot do all this shepherding ourselves, but we need to ensure that all have shepherds.‘

How to Grow Into Christian Leadership

We have looked at three models for Christian leadership, and three ways of assimilating at least part of the biblical material concerning them, to enrich and correct our understanding of leadership. Obviously any of the three approaches can be used beneficially for any of the three models.

Clearly, having the right concepts or knowing the right models in itself doesn't get us very far. Good pictures don't guarantee good leadership, any more than good maps ensure we get to our destination. There were, and still are, bad servants, shepherds, and stewards. So we need to assimilate and integrate what we learn. It needs to become a constant desire that this will happen. We need to be willing to change where necessary. We need to work out what changes are needed. We need to practice these changes and monitor our progress. We need the help of God to break the old patterns of behaviour and attitudes for they are normally rooted very deeply in our personality and conditioning. Our prayer partners are a vital resource from God for our good in this respect. They can help us check our progress, they can be praying for us. Sometimes, through them, God may show us areas of our past or personality that need healing.

More Ways of Growing Into Christian Leadership Through the Bible

There are many other ways in which we can use Scripture to help us develop our Christian leadership. One of the most obvious is through studying the character of biblical leaders. A book like John Eddison's *Understanding Leadership* is a good introduction to several biblical leaders. Or John White's *Excellence in Leadership* which deals specifically with Nehemiah if more detail is required. Another approach is to study different aspects of leadership through books with a biblical perspective such as Andre Le Peau's *Paths of Leadership* or Charles Sibthorpe's *A Man Under Authority*. Calvin Miller's *Leadership* combines the two approaches of studying a biblical character with a thematic approach. David is the chosen character.[7] Yet another approach is through biblical exposition of passages dealing with leadership. A fine chapter to investigate is 1 Thessalonians 2.

Because it is not how much we read but how much we are transformed into better Christian leaders, key questions to face constantly are:

1. Where does this confront or complement my kind of leading?
2. What is the Holy Spirit saying to me through this? What can I learn about my leadership from this?
3. What steps can I take to implement the changes this suggests are necessary?
4. When and how am I going to take these steps?
5. What effect will this have had on my leadership in six months', one year's time?

Inevitably as we become aware of biblical leaders and leadership we discover that with God it is not about styles of leadership, or efficiency in leadership, it is about being the kind of person God wants us to be. To this we now turn our attention.

Tasks

○ 1. Write a parable/story showing a Christian person leading in a non-Christian way and a non-Christian acting in a Christian way.

○ 2. Read a biography of a Christian leader who appeals to you. Appendix B gives a short selection of biographies if you need help here. As you read try to understand why you selected this person. Look for the ways in which their leadership is Christian. If you are in a group you can spend time sharing your insights.

○ × 3. Find some more New Testament models of leadership and seek to understand why they are appropriate for Christian leadership. Can you think of modern equivalents? Philip Greenslade's book has many imaginative suggestions.[8]

○ × 4. Consider ways in which Jesus protected his sheep in the gospels. Try to find at least five ways. Choose two from your list of five that you would like him to do for you. How do you think this would help you in your situations? If you can, share this with your group. If you are leading a group talk to two or three of them and ask them how they would like Christ's/your protection. Try and serve them in these areas during the next month.

○ × 5. Keep a daily log of leadership situations in which you are involved — at home, work, church, leisure. Besides noting the situations record how you felt about them. Did you feel you were being a Christian leader or not? In the light of the New Testament/Christian leadership models, do you think your feelings correspond? What has influenced the way you feel? How Christian are these influences? It will be much more creative if these situations are talked through in the group context.

○ × 6. Share insights you have gained about shepherd, servant, and steward with your prayer partners. Ask them to pray with you and for you in the light of these insights. Share with them any problems this course is generating in your various situations. Ask them to pray for God's solutions. Find a way to express your appreciation to your prayer partners. Remember to find out what needs they have.

References — Chapter 2

1. C P Wagner, *Leading Your Church to Growth* (MARC, 1986), p.82.
2. Peter Nott, "Towards a Theology of Leadership", *Expository Times,* February, 1986, p.139.
3. John Finney, *Understanding Leadership* (Daybreak, 1989).
   Philip King, *Leadership Explosion* (Hodder and Stoughton, 1987).
   Philip Greenslade, *Leadership* (Marshalls Paperbacks, 1984).
4. E.g. see C Ashton, *Servant Spirit — Servant Church* (Marshall Pickering, 1988). The quote is from John Finney, op.cit. pp.58–59.
5. P King, op.cit. p.128; P Greenslade, op.cit. p.106; John Perry, *Effective Christian Leadership* (Hodder, 1987), p.17.
6. C P Wagner, op.cit. pp.58–60.
7. John Eddison, *Understanding Leadership* (Scripture Union, 1974).
   John White, *Excellence in Leadership* (IVP, 1986).
   Andre Le Peau, *Paths of Leadership* (IVP, 1984).
   Charles Sibthorpe, *A Man Under Authority* (Kingsway, 1984).
   Calvin Miller, *Leadership* (Navpress, 1987.
8. See note 3.

CHAPTER 3

BECOMING A MORE EFFECTIVE CHRISTIAN LEADER

"the supreme quality for a leader is unquestionably integrity"[1]

Goal

To begin to develop a more Christian character as the basis for effective Christian leadership.

Aims

1. To understand why character is essential for Christian leadership.
2. To see from experiences in the life of Jesus how God prepares our character for leadership.
3. To see how we can grow from our own ordinary life situations.
4. To look at three character traits which are important for Christian leadership.
5. To begin to develop a lifetime's process of growth.
6. To harness time for prayer as a key factor in this process.

Main Scriptures

Luke 4.1–44; Ephesians 5.21—6.9; 1 Timothy 3.1–13; Titus 1.5–9

Introduction

Here's a riddle:

One was a doctor, and one was a queen,
And one was a shepherd on the green,
One was a soldier, and one was a priest,
And one was slain by a fierce wild beast.

What are they? The answer is easy for those who know the hymn "I sing a song of the saints of God". Although, they were not only saints, they were also leaders among God's people. The hymn goes on to say, quite rightly in my opinion.

And there's not any reason, no, not the least,
Why I shouldn't be one too.

When we review the kind of people who Scripture and church history present as leaders there is no reason why we can't be one too. Each of us is the raw material that God can use to become effective leaders for him. Equally amazing, God seems able to use any and every experience of life to help build us into his kind of leader. Yet to be his kind of leader we must inevitably commit ourselves to growing Christlikeness of character.

There is considerable debate about the right of newspapers to pry into, and report on, the private lives of public people. All of us have sympathy with those who say "leave them alone, they deserve their own life too". But how important the private lives of public people are is a more delicate question. Perhaps it is fairly clear that what matters for test match cricketers is performance on the field but, in so far as they represent their country, doesn't their private behaviour also count, even if it does not adversely affect their performance? Anyway, how does dubious behaviour affect that indefinable, but crucially significant, matter of team spirit? Integrity, reliability and commitment are somehow involved.

What about political leaders? Does it matter if they have "affairs" if their overt political performance is satisfactory? Is their credibility not reduced somewhat? More obviously, if someone leads in sport they must be fit, or if someone is involved in situations where life saving decisions are taken they must be fully alert. Equally, if we are involved in leading people into Christian maturity and effectiveness we must be as Christlike as possible. This is not only for the sake of appearance or integrity, but as a matter of effectiveness. Somehow if that Christlikeness of character does not show through, our effectiveness as Christian leaders is hampered. Although the essentials of Christlikeness of character are not easily defined we need to be the right kind of person, as well as learning to act in a Christian way. Indeed, the more we become involved in Christian leadership the greater the pressures on us to destroy our Christlikeness of character. Paul has some wise words for all, but they are particularly applicable to Christian leaders.

> *Whoever thinks he is standing firm had better be careful that he does not fall. Every test that you have experienced is the kind that normally comes to people. But God keeps his promise, and he will not allow you to be tested beyond your power to remain firm; at the time you are put to the test, he will give you the strength to endure it, and so provide you with a way out. (1 Corinthians 10.12–13)*

In John's Gospel Jesus relates, "I am the vine, and you are the branches. Whoever remains in me, and I in him, will bear much fruit; for you can do nothing without me" John 15.5. Remaining in the vine means allowing the life of the vine to shape us and resource us.

However, before we all resign from our positions or ask for our money back for this book, we are not asked to be perfect before we can lead. None of God's leaders were. In fact Scripture seems to go out of its way to show they were not. In the second half of Mark's Gospel we are presented with a portrait of disaster for Peter who has been declared to be "the rock". But however Peter might fail, Christ would see that Peter developed. What God wants from us is a willingness to be transformed. This process is one which should never end.

Jesus was perfect yet God was perfecting him through his life experiences of suffering and obedience (Hebrews 2.10, 5.7–10). How much more, then, do we need to let God mature us through our life experiences. By looking at a series of incidents in the life of Jesus (Luke 4) we shall see how we can grow through our life situations.

A Chapter in the Life of Jesus — Luke 4.1–44

If we read quickly through this chapter we see that God is building the person of Jesus in three distinct situations:

1. Temptations to misuse his power and position
2. Challenge to, and conflict through, his leadership
3. Pressure from interruptions and popularity

Temptations — Luke 4.1–13

Normally we read these well-known temptation stories as an illustration of the claim of Hebrews 4.15, "We have a High Priest who was tempted in every way that we are, but did not sin".

Thus, the temptation to turn stones into bread is the temptation to satisfy our bodily appetites, that of seeing all the world's kingdoms as a form of avarice or possessiveness, and jumping from the temple as attention seeking. There is a relevance in all of this that we cannot dispute. However, the temptations are more penetrating once we see them as Jesus struggling with the various ways of using his messianic powers. They are fundamentally about ways of leading. Should he lead by miraculously satisfying human physical needs and desires? Should he lead by using satanic methods of fear, hatred and division, or even political power? Should he lead by appealing to the desire for amusement and amazement? In some ways he might have been more effective, particularly in the short term, in building a following using any or all of these approaches. But clearly it would no longer be a form of Christian leadership!

In passing, it is worth noting that Jesus needed the illumination of Scripture to reveal the lie in the heart of these inappropriate ways, and so shall we. Struggling with approaches it is rarely clear to us, unaided, where God's way goes. We need constantly to be checking our methods and motives as leaders. Most of us find it helpful if our leadership is open to the careful scrutiny of others. If we belong to a group it is worth discussing together ways in which we can experience the same kind of temptations to misapply our Christian leadership.

Confrontation, Challenge and Conflict — Luke 4.14–30

As if to confirm the real nature of the temptations, Jesus' next reported action is to declare positively his messianic leadership and his manifesto. We can take note of some important features:

1. Jesus was clear about his task, his resources for the task, his source of authorization for the task, and the ways in which this clashed with the expectations of those around him.
2. People were impressed with his leadership gifts (verse 22) but were also looking for ways of undermining his standing (verse 22b). We need to learn how to cope with such gibes. Jesus does not get entangled by irrelevant and diverting comments. He redirects and affirms his message.
3. Jesus was unable to pacify his critics. We should remember Paul's directive "...always aim at those things that bring peace and that help to strengthen one another" (Romans 14.19). But Jesus could not always avoid conflict and nor shall we.

However, Jesus rightly shows us the importance of keeping to the issues of the nature of God's kingdom and of avoiding arguments of a personal nature.

4. We see that Jesus had to cope with severe and destructive anger directed towards him because of what he stood for. Here he was able to move away unscathed. Ultimately he would not be able to do so. Again it is worth spending some time thinking about, or preferably discussing with others, ways of coping with anger and resentment. Could Jesus legitimately have avoided this confrontation? When is it right to pacify? On my wall I have a quotation, "The Holy Spirit came not only to comfort the afflicted, but to afflict the comfortable".

Pressures for Leaders — Luke 4.31–41

Perhaps he went to Capernaum for an easier time. After all it was there his miracles (4.23) and words (4.32) were well received. If so, it was not to be. In the synagogue, again trouble threatened him. This time in the form of a demonic power confrontation. Now his ability to deal with the unexpected leads to greater pressure. At Simon's home he is again in demand because Simon's mother-in-law is ill. Soon sunset comes, and with it a crowd of people with all kinds of needs, draining still further the resources and the patience of Jesus. Does 4.42 "At daybreak" indicate he has been coping all night? Even when he seeks for solitude with his Father the people pursue him.

Today, leaders face pressures from the telephone, from the demands for further training, from the complexities of modern needs, from the person-starving nature of our society (and we can add our own). So often when we feel we can cope with no more, those we depend on, friends and family especially, become a source of pressure instead of help. When we try and find time for our own spiritual resourcing that goes wrong too. Jesus knew it all. We need to build up our capacity to cope (1 Corinthians 9.25–27). We need to recognize our pressure times as an opportunity for God to strengthen us (James 1.12–14). We can remember that he has promised "...not to allow you to be tested beyond your power to remain firm; at the time you are put to the test, he will give you the strength to endure it..." (1 Corinthians 10.13). However, we are not to "put the Lord our God to the test" by deliberately seeking out situations and pressures unnecessarily and unceasingly.

Please make a list of the pressures you have to cope with using table 2 — daily, weekly and less often. Ask God to show you what he can accomplish in you through these situations. Hard as it is, it is helpful to thank God for them, for his presence with you in them and for his promise that he will work in them to bring good out of them. Where you can't see that possibility ask him to show you as

TABLE 2

	Daily	Weekly	Less often	What God wants to do for me	How far is he succeeding (0 – 5)
Family					
Work					
Community					
Leisure					
Church					

you live through these situations during the next few weeks and months. As God shows you his will it might be helpful to use the last two columns of the chart. It is good to keep coming back to this.

The great thing about Jesus is that he did not allow the pressures and demands of people, sensitive and responsive as he was to them, to deflect him from his God-given priorities. Was this because he could draw on the resources of resolved temptations, accepted constantly the empowering of God's Spirit and valued the disciplines of fasting and prayer?

It is important that we review the pressure we are under and ascertain whether they are really necessary, or partly self-induced. It is equally important we are learning to use all the legitimate resources that God provides. Incidentally, how helpful are prayer partners proving to be? Are we making the best use of them to help us grow into Christlike leadership?

Three Character Traits to "Go for Growth"

There are many Christlike character features that, as leaders, we desire for ourselves. For the moment we shall look at three which are frequently highlighted in Scripture. They are humility, compassion and loyalty/courage. Jesus said "...Learn from me, because I am gentle and humble in spirit, ..." (Matthew 11.29).

Humility

Paul says of Jesus "He was humble..." (Philippians 2.8). His humility was expressed in his becoming man, in his human life and, ultimately, in his sacrificial death. The counterpoint of humility is obedience. "He was humble and walked the path of obedience..." (Philippians 2.8). Jesus claimed he only did what he was told by the Father. Because he knew his life was completely for God he was able to live freely and without any need to claim status, praise, honour, or attention for himself. His humility left him free to welcome outcasts or children without the slightest concern for his reputation. His humility made him a leader who was easy to approach and attractive to follow. Humility is one of the marks of a great leader. For Jesus, a great source of humility was knowing who he was. He knew he was the Son of God, he knew who his Father was and he knew his Father knew too! Out of this ultimate security his humility was sustained and natural. Paul not only says

"He was humble", he says "...be humble towards one another..." (Philippians 2.3). He indicates two ways in which that humility can grow. First, "consider others better than yourselves". This does not mean we are to belittle ourselves but that we are to (over) value others. We can grow in humility by developing an ability to appreciate the good in others (cf. Philippians 4.8–9), and genuinely and openly affirming that good. Because of who we are (children of God) and because of what we are about (obeying God) we are free to do this. Supremely, of course, we recognize that good in Jesus.

Secondly, we grow in humility by "looking out for one another's interests". This means really wanting other people's plans to work out, helping them achieve their aims, supporting them in their endeavour, whether or not they reciprocate. It means recognizing that what seems trivial to us, and in terms of the kingdom strategy may indeed be so, if it is important to others it needs to be accepted on other people's significance scale. Everyday life provides us with an endless stream of opportunities to practise this — from the dinner table to the boardroom table, from the washing machine to the car, from getting up to going to bed. But we want more. We want to have "the attitude of Christ Jesus". Paul indicates that to gain this we need to be focusing on Jesus (Philippians 2.5–11). There is the wonderful promise that as we do this "...the Lord, who is the Spirit, transforms us into his likeness in an ever greater degree of glory." (2 Corinthians 3.18)

We need to desire his heart but we also need to practise his art. The two go hand in hand. When we fail in deed or spirit then we need "to humble ourselves under God's mighty hand" (1 Peter 5.6) so we can be renewed in our pursuit of humility.

Compassion

One of the unusual and distinctive qualities attributed to Jesus is that of compassion, or as the *Good News Bible* tends to translate it "a heart filled with pity". The Greek word is *splagchnizesthai.* Its origin is rather lowly. It is used for the inside parts of a sacrifice, especially the intestines — the lower, less highly thought of inner parts! But it has come to mean something truly powerful and noble. Although the word is similar to having mercy and showing kindness the distinctiveness in application to Jesus is noteworthy. It reminds us of the extra dimension, deeper quality and richer response that we, as Christian leaders, should cultivate and allow God to give us. Being leaders should not make us harder, less sensitive, or better cushioned. Being leaders should not mean we learn to hide our feelings of tenderness and cover up our emotional response with hard self control. If we look to Christ the reverse is the case. Leading means being willing to feel more, and to feel more deeply. To allow that feeling to be communicated to others and to allow it to motivate us into action. For compassion is not only feeling, it is feeling such a power of caring, we desire to do something to help.

Although in the Gospels it is only used of Jesus, Jesus does use it of others in three parables. Two of them clarify these points. Luke 15.20 helps us sense the intensity and quality of the emotion. Here the word is used of the father of the prodigal son after all the years of anxious waiting. "He (the prodigal son) was still a long way from home when his father saw him; *his heart was filled with pity,* and he ran, threw his arms round his son…"

The father's love is so overwhelming he completely disregards his own dignity and runs, because he is completely focused on his son, not himself. This quality of compassion is possible only for those who temporarily (in the father's case) or permanently (in Jesus' case) have crucified self. We can also see that this compassion communicates — he threw his arms round his son, and all the rest. It not only feels deeply, it wants the other to experience and be bathed in the feelings.

The second parable is equally well known — the Good Samaritan. We read about his response to the wounded and robbed traveller. "…when he saw him, *his heart was filled with pity.* He went over to him, poured oil and wine on his wounds and bandaged them…" (Luke 10.33–34). Here the powerful feeling is generated by the other's need. Because of compassion the Samaritan disregards his own security and acts sacrificially to alleviate the need.

In the four main references to Jesus showing compassion we can discern these same dynamics. Jesus displays freedom to feel deeply because of others' needs, ability to communicate that feeling to others and commitment to action to rectify the needs (Matthew 9.36; 14.14; 15.32; 20.34).

How can we become more compassionate? Compassion is the partner of love. So above all we need to ask God to give to us his heart of love. First for ourselves, then for the people and situations we face either immediately, that is in face to face encounters, or less directly through the media or other forms of learning. Such a prayer carries a health warning. As we invite God, through the

Holy Spirit, to pour his love for others into our hearts we shall need to become more open and receptive to receiving God's love for ourselves. We may need to repent that we still have a heart of stone and instead long for that living, warm, heart of flesh that God promises (Ezekiel 36.26). Cheap emotion is no substitute. Compassion is penetrating, both in terms of understanding the real needs of the person who calls forth the compassion and in the demands it places on those who show it. Yet undoubtedly it is the hallmark of a growing Christian leader.

Loyalty/Courage

An undeniable quality of the leadership of Jesus is his courage. It radiates all through the Gospels — walking through the crowd at Nazareth, facing the demented demoniac of Gadara, defending others from the scathing attack of the Pharisees, deflating a Galilean storm, facing the brutality of enraged leaders, risking his friendships because of his commitment to the truth. His courage was also contagious. When the members of the Sanhedrin were seeking to immobilize Peter and John they "...were amazed to see how bold Peter and John were and to learn that they were ordinary men of no education. They realized then that they had been companions of Jesus." (Acts 4.13)

To be courageous does not mean there will be no reluctance to face the enemy nor that there is a desire to self-destruct. The courage that Jesus displayed arose out of his absolute commitment to the Father's will. Peter and John were probably fearful of the fate that might await them. They were courageous in the sense of being unswerving in their openness and dedication to Christ's cause.

How can we grow in our boldness? Partly by ensuring our commitment is resolute. Partly by ensuring we spend time with Jesus. Partly by doing what the disciples did — praying for it and partly by doing it when the opportunity arises. Next time we feel fear arising we can take it as an opportunity to grow in boldness. First, check out that we are sure what we are doing and why. Secondly, invite the Holy Spirit to control our emotional and physical panic symptoms. Thirdly, recall who we are — children of God — and the authority that comes with that. Finally, act and speak firmly and confidently even if we are not feeling like it. When we come through the situation, then we remember where the boldness came from and give thanks to God. This way boldness grows.

These three character traits can be seen in Luke Chapter 4. In the temptations Jesus was humbling himself under God when he brought in Scripture. In Nazareth he announced his ministry of compassion and in Capernaum he practised it. In Nazareth, both in his words to the synagogue congregation and in his actions, he displayed his courage. These three character traits are significant in another way. The servant needs, above all, humility. Jesus "...took the nature of a servant... He was humble" (Philippians 2.7–8). The shepherd needs compassion. It was when Jesus saw the crowd with a shepherd's eyes, "...like sheep without a shepherd", that he was filled with pity for them (Matthew 9.36). The steward needs loyalty/courage to ensure that his master's plans and possessions are protected against all threats. These three areas of growth are essential for those who would become more effective Christian leaders.

A Lifetime's Process

This process of growth in Christian character needs constant attention, like keeping fit. At times of greatest pressure we need to be fittest. Two of the greatest Christian leaders, Luther and Wesley, both affirmed that the busier they were the more time they needed to devote to prayer. Most of us cry out "How can we find more time for prayer?" There is value in carving out time for prayer, even out of our "sleep time", but there are many other opportunities we can grasp "to buy back the time". Waiting at traffic lights or in traffic jams we need no longer feel frustrated, we can pray. Queuing at the supermarket or DSS we can pray. Doing routine tasks that don't really demand all our faculties — peeling potatoes, cleaning the car — we can pray. We can also use the situation we are in to stimulate our praying — patience when queuing, thankfulness when preparing meals, confession when cleaning the car, and a thousand others as the Spirit suggests to us.

We also need to check out our day with God. It is helpful to go over our day with God last thing at night. I find this especially helpful when I think I have achieved little. God usually shows me he has accomplished more than I knew. But we also need to learn where we went wrong, how things could have been less difficult, how we need to be different and so on. Conversely we need to learn to share the coming day with God; to invite him into our plans; to allow him to direct us even in our dress or make up if he wants; to ask him for his guidance and provision. Then when we enter difficult situations we shall know he is there and act accordingly. These are a few simple, practical ways of giving the Holy Spirit space to produce his fruit in us (read Galatians 5.22–23).

In this chapter we have stressed the importance of character, Christlike character, for effective Christian leadership. However character is not enough. We also need to know how best to "do the job". To this we now turn — and may character continue to grow!

Growth Opportunities

Tasks

○ ✕ 1. Make a list of the ways Jesus would have been "made perfect" through the experiences recorded in Luke 4. Can you think of ways in which these experiences strengthened him for even more demanding, but parallel, experience in his later ministry? Can you see a similar learning experience for each of the growth points for Jesus? Are you aware of aspects of your personality which need developing? Can you ask for God to build you up in these areas?

○ ✕ 2. Consider going on retreat or learning to fast and pray to provide an opportunity for God to review your leadership with you. How can you do these things? What problems might you expect?

○ △ 3. By working through *The Measure of a Man/Woman*[2], or by reading scriptures about the fruit of the Spirit or the qualities of a leader:

   i) Pick out three areas of character where you are strong
   ii) Pick out two areas of character where you are weak
   iii) Pick out two areas of character where you would like to improve (i.e. not your strong nor your weak areas, but aspects of Christian character where you have some strength but see value in, and room for, considerable improvement)

   Then:

   i) Check with people who know you whether your perceptions are the same as theirs
   ii) Work out targets/exercises for the two areas where you would like to improve
   iii) Involve prayer partners in prayer for two areas where you are weak

Check progress in three months. Then work out exercises to strengthen etc. as for (ii)

○ 4. Write a diary for the end and beginning of each day and review with God thanks/confession/help.

○ 5. Keep a careful review of the "dead minutes" you can utilize for prayer. Check each day how well you are doing.

References — Chapter 3

1. D Eisenhower, quoted in A Le Peau, *Paths of Leadership* (IVP, 1984), p.89.
2. G A Getz, *The Measure of a Man/Woman* (Regal, 1974/1977).

CHAPTER 4

WAYS OF LEADING AS A CHRISTIAN

"The Queen was in a furious passion, and went stamping about, and shouting 'Off with his head!' or 'Off with her head!' about once a minute."[1]

Goal

To use secular insights to widen the selection of leadership styles appropriate for Christians.

Aims

1. To introduce the reader to the various styles of leadership available and to consider some disadvantages.
2. To consider how far and in what kind of situations these styles can be a Christian option.
3. To increase awareness of the leaders' own preferred styles.
4. To encourage greater width of leadership styles so we can select the most appropriate.

Main Scriptures

Luke 23.

"...because the Church is a human institution as well as a divine one the insights of sociology can be valuable in understanding how it operates." So writes Philip King in his introduction to, and recommendation of, the use of different styles of leadership in the Christian context.[2]

Our first response may well be "Can this be right?" Should we use secular styles in our Christian work? I think that because secular leadership has to work and because it has been so thoroughly scrutinized we, as Christian leaders, can learn a great deal. I also think Jesus supports this approach! Remember that we saw that "steward" was a significant biblical model for us. Jesus had this to say at the end of one of his parables about a manager "…the people of this world are much more shrewd in handling their affairs than the people who belong to the light." (Luke 16.8) Jesus was encouraging his disciples to learn from the secular world. Indeed, in using pictures of servants and shepherds Jesus was utilizing secular styles for himself and his followers. Of course neither Jesus nor we can simply take things over, we must "Put all things to the test: keep what is good and avoid every kind of evil." (1 Thessalonians 5.21–22)

But we should also look fearlessly at the insights of secular leadership. Doing so alerts us; using this approach we can easily be "squeezed into the world's mould". However, it also helps us see that this has probably already happened to us by "absorption". So the very challenge of filtering what is acceptable from secular approaches can help us be less conformist ourselves.

First then, let us look at this absorption process. My natural inclination is to think that the democratic style of leadership is more Christian. We should consult one another because we are brothers and sisters, we should respect one another's views. If the Holy Spirit is given to all believers then God may speak through any of us. Conversely, leaders who act with heavy authority appear to be lording it over us, domineering not gentle, imposing their views rather than recognizing God's will.

To me, then, the democratic way seems naturally Christian; I am comfortable with this style of leadership. However, when I reflect on this I begin to see that much of this comfort is because it fits in with the secular ways in which I have been brought up. I have been nurtured in a democratic society whose values are all around me for me to absorb and whose principles have been drip fed to me through the educational and social system. Even my nonconformist church tradition was profoundly influenced by the growth of democracy. As a Baptist, where the ultimate decision making body is the church meeting, open to all members, it is encouraging to see other denominations moving towards more open processes of decision making, for example the growing power of Parochial Church Councils, and more participation in Anglican decision making at every level. It affirms my sense of the appropriateness of the democratic leader.

Besides, I am aware that the kind of person I am favours the democratic style. I have a sense of fairness, much of me is gentle and does not want to enforce my views on others (mind you, I do want them "voluntarily" to agree I am right!). I do value other people and affirm their worth. But I soon realize that not all that makes democracy appealing to me is necessarily Christian. I need people's approval and esteem — the more the better. I do want to avoid conflict. I prefer discussion to decision; I find the former stimulating and less demanding than decisions which commit me to action.

Now, I am aware that the social and personal features which attract me to democracy may not apply to you! You may be quite angry with my arrogant assumption that democracy is Christian. You may see "sheep without a shepherd" needing decisive, directive leadership, which you can provide. You may know that people respond to vision and confidence and you may find great fulfilment in providing it and seeing what needs doing done with the minimum of fuss. Perhaps you are trained to lead.

Through Boy Scouts or Girls' Brigade, as a policeman or office manager, as a foreman or a director, or as a clergyman, you know that you can provide the leadership people readily respond to. You have been given authority to act and to impose certain decisions so you know the value of a degree of autocratic leadership. Maybe you have read the Scriptures so you know that the divine structure is not democratic. God did not consult with Adam and Eve concerning the forbidden status of the tree of knowledge, he told them. Jesus did not invite his followers to select twelve representative apostles, he chose them. Looking around it is easy to see the damaging effects of democracy on our society. Weakness in management leads to the demise of great industries. The growth of the house church movement shows the benefits of "real" leadership and the necessity of authority to sustain growth, creative development, and satisfaction among Christian people.

Whether your feelings are with me, with those who value strong leadership, or somewhere in the middle, is not the main issue of this chapter. Rather, it is to help us all be more aware of the wide range of styles available and to help us assess the merits of them.

> *It is all too easy to assume that the style we know best, the one we have used in the past or the one that most suits our personality, is the best or preferred one.*[3]

There are many contemporary attempts to analyze leadership styles. Table 3 is a diagrammatic representation with some comments. I use three main categories, namely authoritarian, democratic, permissive. However, there is really a spectrum, not a series of steps, and most people will use a mixed style, even in a single given context.

Comments

The Commitment of the Group to the Decision

This is influenced by many factors other than the style of leadership and this is particularly true in the Christian context. Some of these factors are:

1. The group's commitment to the overall purpose and the extent to which they perceive any decision furthers that purpose.
2. The group's commitment to the leader as a person — because of his position i.e. appointed by God, because of past experience and proven results.
3. The perceived importance of the decision. The more important the decision the more a mature group will want to be involved in the decision, the less important the less a mature group will want to be involved.
4. The urgency of the decision. The more urgent the more willing most groups will be to accept the decision e.g. "Get out of the building now, it's on fire".
5. The maturity of the group. By maturity I mean the level of faith and gift development, the level of trust between members (including the leader) which involves the individual's sense of security and self worth.

Sub-division of the Three Styles

Authoritarian

This can include:

1. Autocratic — imposes their will on the group. Able to do this because of their powerful personality or their position. Authority is claimed by the person.
2. Charismatic — acts independently, expects others to follow. People often do follow because of the attractiveness of the person rather than any critical assessment of the policies and decisions. Authority is given to the person.
3. Traditional — here the base for the approach is not personal

Type of Leader

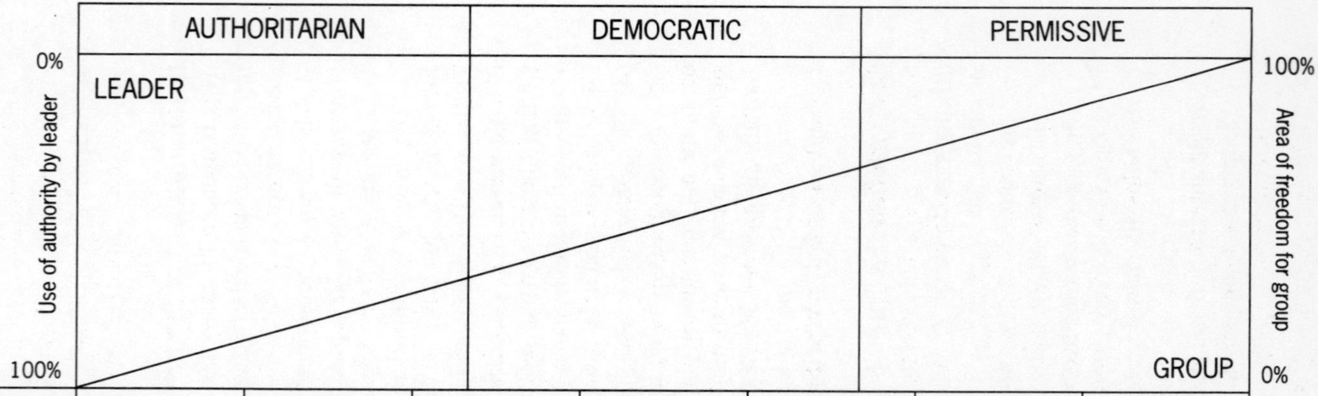
AUTHORITARIAN
DEMOCRATIC
PERMISSIVE
0%
Use of authority by leader
100%
LEADER
GROUP
100%
Area of freedom for group
0%

Leader's style	Makes decisions Announces them **TELLS**	Makes decisions Explains them **SELLS**	Makes and receives suggestions Leader takes decisions **CONSULTS**	Defines limits of group's input. Joins group & makes decisions with group **SHARES**	Allows others to function within limits Leader gives and group accepts **DELEGATES**	Allows others to decide what to decide **RESIGNS**	Doesn't mind whether anything is decided or not **ABANDONS**
Commitment of group to decisions	Low	Low	High	High	High	Low	What decisions?
Commitment of group to leader	Low – High	Medium – High	Medium	Medium	Medium	Low	Low

power or attractiveness but appeal to the higher authority — tradition and the ability to justify procedures in the light of this. Authority is derived by the person.

4. Mechanistic — here the power base is the ability to ensure the product is efficiently and consistently produced and to control people and plans through attention to detail. Authority is earned by the person.

Democratic

1. Human relations — response to other human beings within the group and an ability to integrate and harmonize their views and energies is the main feature of this style.
2. Professional or organic — response to the needs of those outside the group and the changing environment are the main features of this. But it is still a form of democracy!

Permissive

This is not often dealt with in management books, but in practice is quite prevalent in churches. The main function of such leadership is to help the group survive with the minimum of disturbance. The group doesn't have any significant functions external to itself. I think two kinds can be distinguished — protective and introspective. The protective leader does the utmost to keep outside pressures from impinging on the group but leaves the group free to be, or do, or not. The introspective leader fields the inter-group tension and is often some form of scapegoat. The caricatures of father and mother correspond to these two forms.

Evaluation of the Three Styles

Authoritarian

Some of the evaluative features depend on which of the four subdivisions are dominant. In general, however:

Advantages

Decisions can be taken quickly and decisively. They can be action centred and effective for crisis response.
It provides security for people.
It helps members learn obedience and discipline.

Disadvantages

Depends on one person. Group can be immobilized if leader is removed.

Leader can become egotistical and isolated, detracts from dependence and obedience to God.
Restricts the input of insight and information.
Members become fearful and maturity is not developed.
Tends to reduce commitment of the group to the task.
Leads to build-up of resentment and hostility and ultimately splintering.

Democratic

Advantages
Strong group commitment to accepted tasks and one another.
Develops caring relationship for group members.
Builds up gifts, individuality and maturity.
Sustainable in the absence of the main leader.
Many people involved in listening and responding to God.

Disadvantages
Reaching and carrying out decisions can be a slow process.
Discussion can degenerate into disagreement or become an excuse for inactivity.
Individuals can drift out of the group; the less able and less vocal can easily become demoralized.
God's views can be replaced by the group's wishes and whims.
Requires considerable maturity by the members and the leader to remain effective.

Permissive

Advantages
Everyone can be accepted and affirmed.
There need not be conflict, at least initially.
People can discover their abilities and talents without pressure.
Tends to be person centred which has a Christian feel to it.

Disadvantages
Lack of goals and agreed procedures.
Lack of satisfaction and fulfilment and unity.
Hostility can develop and be expressed within the group destructively.

Group can become dominated by a strong figure and is vulnerable to an authoritarian takeover.
Unlikely to be concerned about God's mission to the world or to accept sacrifice as necessary.
Can easily fall apart because it depends on felt relationships.

With our three main categories in mind we can look at Luke 23. Here, in theory, Pilate and Herod are in positions of great authority but because they are fearful of the consequences they try and avoid antagonizing the crowd and so their leadership style becomes, at times, very permissive. There is a sense of confusion and injustice around. Important decisions needed to be taken and were not, so a serious miscarriage of justice takes place. Behind the pressure of the crowd lies some kind of democratic decision by the Council (see verses 1 and 51). They acted as a group even though not all the members had agreed. We can see here the tremendous power of a united democracy even in the face of absolute authority (verse 20). We have all witnessed this in the changes in the Iron Curtain countries. In the action of soldiers at various times we can see authoritarian leadership at work (verses 11, 26, 36) although their authority is derived. But as a group they act democratically (verse 34).

Joseph of Arimathea acts decisively but he has to work democratically by persuading Pilate to allow him to have the body of Jesus. In a different way the women act democratically. They agree together what needs to be done and get on and do it. Jesus is apparently powerless but he is the one with authority (verses 9, 34, 43), a point made much more strongly in John's account (John 18.28–40). In one sense this chapter shows the success and the ultimate failure of democracy, the crowd get their way so Jesus is crucified; of authority, because it is in the hands of the crowd and fails miserably; and of permissiveness because opting out of leadership allowed Jesus to die.

No style guarantees success. It also shows how interactive these styles are in any given situation. Here are some more biblical passages worth examining for leadership styles. Exodus 32; 1 Samuel 17; 1 Kings 12.1–20; Jeremiah 38; Acts 6.1–7; Acts 15. Perhaps you would like to select your own biblical examples of leadership styles:

Authoritarian e.g.

Democratic e.g.

Permissive e.g.

What do I Like Best?

It is important that we understand what our preference in leadership style is and why. We can gain insight into this by reflecting on how we operate in different contexts and when we seem most at ease. It is worth checking our views with people who know us; Pilate probably thought he was authoritarian but his wife and the Sanhedrin knew better!

It is also worth considering what kinds of leadership we admire. What does our choice in biography suggest? What kind of secular leadership do we like or dislike? Which leaders on TV do we find ourselves drawn to and why? What kind of leaders do we like working with?

Don't be surprised if the answers point in different directions. We are complex beings. The way we think we should act might contrast with our natural style, or the way we have been trained, or the most appropriate style in a given situation, or the way the Holy Spirit is gifting us. All these features might show through as we reflect on our preferences in different contexts and, indeed, such a variety can become a servant of the kingdom. Nevertheless many of us will become aware of a style which we use most frequently, or feel most comfortable with, or think is best. We should also examine, preferably with the help of others, whether, and under what conditions, we change from one style to another. Pilate moved out of his authoritarian style because he was afraid of the Sanhedrin. Sometimes we may also move because we are being manipulated. Such changes will lead to unfairness, lack of direction, and confusion among those being led.

Developing our Menu

There is great variety in the ways people lead. No one style has all the virtues, even from a Christian viewpoint. We may be "in touch" with several ways of leading within ourselves, even though we have a dominant style. Although such variety can be detrimental it can also provide us with a resource for developing our choice of styles so that we can serve God, and his people, in the best way through the most appropriate leadership style.

In order to do this as Christians we need to grasp clearly two fundamental points. First, whatever style we use, all our authority is derived from God and we can never be free to either dominate others or surrender to them. "We are your servants for Christ's sake." We are shepherds under the direction of the chief shepherd etc. Secondly, our leadership style must itself be a form of service. This must mean that at times we must lay aside our preferred style in order to best serve God and the group we are called to lead.

With God's help we can extend our preferred style. For instance, we may normally be uncomfortable with the authoritarian style although we recognize we sometimes use it with our children and they respond reasonably well. "Wash your hands, dinner's ready", "Please turn off the TV and get on with your homework" etc. As we reflect on this we may discover that one reason we don't like the authoritarian style, either sitting under or using it, is that it seems like a parent–child relationship, not an adult–adult one. However if we bring other factors into account we may feel freer to transfer this style to an adult context. We may realize we use it because they accept us as leaders and know from many other factors that we love them and value them. We may realize it saves lengthy, repetitive and unproductive negotiations if they are sure we mean what we say. We may realize we use it, not to dominate, but to provide security or when danger threatens ("Get back from the cliff edge!"). We may then see there are some adult situations which would benefit from a more directive kind of leadership, (it might equally be that we try out some less authoritarian approaches with our children too!); for example, where there is a strong sense of mutual respect, where people have asked us to give a strong lead, where discussions are repetitive and unproductive, or where avoidance techniques are being used by some.

As we try to transfer styles we may initially feel uncomfortable. We should not be too easily put off, nor be too easily convinced the new style is working better. We need to ask the Holy Spirit to show us when to use different styles and seek to be surrendered to God so he can use our resources. We should involve other people in monitoring the results and talk to those in the group about whether they found it helpful or not. If we are changing our style of leadership in the direction of our personal preference then obviously we need to be especially careful that we are not doing so to satisfy ourselves rather than serve the group.

As we involve God in the process of developing our style of leadership we may also come to see that our secular job or life style is affecting the way we lead in our Christian contexts. Sometimes this is because our personality (which is God given but which also needs to be restored) fits us for that secular style. But we do need to be alert that this secular process is not misfitting us for our Christian leadership. It can be helpful to ask Christian friends to talk these issues through with us. Anyway, God may want to free us for other ways of leading. Equally, if our secular position imposes a style on us with which we are not comfortable then we may "bounce back" to the other end of the spectrum in our leisure or Christian context. This may be an occasional phenomenon as well as a perennial one — we may be less tolerant and patient if we have had a bad day at the office, or wherever! We will want God's help to ensure that any "bounce back" is what God wants for us and those we lead, or we will need his help to handle it. But openness with those who lead with us, or those we lead, can be a beneficial way of proceeding here.

As we develop our abilities to lead in different ways God will help us become aware of who we are, of what the situations require and of what is more helpful to the people we lead. He can help us become more flexible in our leadership styles, and therefore freer to help people through our Christian leadership. In the process we will become more complete as people and more appreciated as leaders because we will be serving in a more sacrificial way. But leadership is not only about allowing God to develop appropriate styles, it is also about the gifting of the Holy Spirit and to the issues and opportunities which this raises we now turn.

Tasks

○ × 1. Consider situations and determine (preferably in a group) where on the leadership styles spectrum the leadership fits and why. Everyday e.g. dentist *vis–à–vis* nurse and patient, family deciding how to spend a "day off". Church e.g. choir practice, organist, choir leader, choir members (minister); worship leader during service *vis–à–vis* congregation; pastoral counselling. How else could these situations be led? What are the differences which different leadership styles might generate?

× 2. Group role play exercise.
Attempt the same task with three different leadership styles. If there are enough people instruct each group to work with one style. If the group is mature enough the impact will be experienced more vividly if only the leader in each group knows which style they are to use.
e.g. Plan a day trip for the church (or part of it).
Redecorate a room at church (in theory only!).
Decide on a new hymn/song book for the church and plan how to introduce it.

○ × 3. Talk with people whom you lead. Ask them how you make them feel, e.g. do they like being with you, do you give them confidence? How helpful you are, e.g. do you explain things clearly, do you support them when things are difficult, do you get in the way? What kind of leaders do they like to follow?
People we might ask: our children, spouses, team members, i.e. colleagues at work or within groups in the church.

○ 4. Every day we are taking decisions small and large. For three days note as many decisions as possible which you take. Try and spot how you make those decisions (which leadership style do you use), why you make the decisions that way. Do you think taking the decisions a different

way would affect the outcome? For the next three days, with selected issues, use a different style and assess the outcome. (Will you do this alone or involve others?)
e.g. You decide where to get the petrol, ask the children.
You decide what to cook for dinner, ask your spouse.
Children choose TV programmes between 5–7pm, have a family conference etc.

○ ✕ 5. Consider situations or groups in your church which you think go well. What kind of leadership is being exercised and how significant is this? Consider a situation in your church where things are not going as well as they might. How significant is the leadership style? How can people support the leadership to help it be more effective?

○ ✕ 6. Devise a Christian obedience training exercise for either children, teenagers, or adults (this can be in the form of a game), and learn from the experience. In what ways does the word "Christian" influence what you do? In groups try out the exercise with adults and monitor results.

References — Chapter 4
1. Lewis Carroll, *Alice in Wonderland* and *Through the Looking Glass* (Dent & Sons, 1954), p.71.
2. P King, *Leadership Explosion* (Hodder and Stoughton, 1987), p.15.
3. Ibid. p.28.

CHAPTER 5

LEADERSHIP AND THE GIFTS OF THE HOLY SPIRIT

I do not think there is any dimension of the Christian life that more effectively joins the teaching of Scripture with the day-to-day activities of the people of God than spiritual gifts.[1]

Goal

To understand the relevance of the gifts of the Spirit for leadership in today's Church.

Aims

1. To introduce us to the biblical material on the gifts of the Holy Spirit and some contemporary accounts.
2. To make further study possible by reference to more detailed treatments of this subject.
3. To consider the inter-relationship between leadership and gifts.
4. To reflect on the relevance of the gifts of the Holy Spirit for leadership in today's Church.
5. To decide which gifts are appropriate for which kinds of leadership.

Main Scriptures

1 Corinthians 12–14; Romans 12.3–8; 1 Peter 4.10–11; Ephesians 4.11–12

Introduction

Fertilizer can be a great asset to farmers. Applied properly to the land it enables them to produce better crops at cheaper costs, which means the consumer pays less for the goods. However, fertilizer can be washed off the soil and, through the rivers and seas, become part of the food chain until eventually it can affect our health negatively. But whether we think fertilizer is a good or bad thing we cannot avoid altogether its effect on our lives.

In a similar way the charismatic movement has affected the well-being of all the churches. Some would see that it has helped the churches "to produce better crops", others would be more conscious of some of the unfortunate side effects. One thing we cannot deny is that it has broadly and deeply influenced the whole Church of Jesus Christ. One such contribution is to highlight the issue of the gifts of the Spirit for Christian people today. Hence we will now assess the contribution that these gifts might make to our Christian leadership. But first, it is helpful to consider the biblical connection between God's Spirit and leadership among God's people.

The Spirit and Leadership

Scripturally, it is clear that even Jesus received the Spirit prior to his ministry. Luke 4 indicates this. First, Luke refers back to Jesus' baptism. "Jesus returned from the Jordan full of the Holy Spirit…" (Luke 4.1). At his baptism Jesus was clothed in the Holy Spirit and immediately following is the declaration that He is God's "own dear Son" with whom God is pleased. The Holy Spirit is involved in the preparation and confirmation of Jesus as a leader.

Next Luke tells us that Jesus "…was led by the Spirit into the desert…" (Luke 4.1) In an undefinable way the testing of Jesus by Satan was a necessary prelude to his ministry. The Spirit was at the heart of this process too. The testing and clarification of the mode and style of leadership is the Spirit's work.

Following his temptations "…Jesus returned to Galilee, and the power of the Holy Spirit was with him." (Luke 4.14) This affects his teaching and the response of the people bear witness to his gifting. Jesus himself was aware of the Spirit's importance for his life. Jesus reads from the scroll of Isaiah in the synagogue at Nazareth. "The Spirit of the Lord is upon me, because he has chosen me to bring good news to the poor… recovery of sight to the blind…" (Luke 4.18). Thus his mighty deeds, as well as his teaching, are dependent on the Spirit's selection.

Jesus' reference to Isaiah 61.1–2 reminds us that there is a strong connection between the Spirit and leadership in the Old Testament. The Spirit is there seen as the source of the call and equipping of the judges. Of Othniel we read "The spirit of the Lord came upon him, and he became Israel's leader." (Judges 3.10) Prior to one of Gideon's daring exploits we read "The spirit of the Lord took control of Gideon…" (Judges 6.34). Second level leaders too are affected by God's Spirit. Moses is addressed by God, "…I will take some of the spirit I have given you and give it to them. Then they can help you bear the responsibility…" (Numbers 11.17). This shows that Moses' leadership was seen to be dependent on God's Spirit and although those who received his Spirit were already recognized as leaders, something was added to them by God's Spirit.

The messianic king was also to be equipped by God's Spirit. Isaiah 11.1–2 is probably the best known statement on this: "…a new king will arise… The spirit of the Lord will give him wisdom, and the knowledge and skill to rule his people…"

The New Testament also knows of this special relationship between the gifting of the Spirit and leadership. For instance, when the early Church selects people to assist the apostles with administrative and welfare matters the apostles direct the people, "…choose seven men among you who are known to be full of the Holy Spirit and wisdom, and we will put them in charge of this matter." (Acts 6.3). Thus there is no doubt that Scripture frequently recognizes a connection between the Holy Spirit and leadership among God's people.

However, not all great leaders in the Bible seem to recognize this fact. Nehemiah is a great spiritual leader who achieved much for God's people but there is no mention of the Holy Spirit in connection with his leadership, even though the prayer of Chapter 9 recognizes the importance of God's Spirit (9.20, 30 — see RSV). Indeed, not even all the prophets relate their activity to God's Spirit. This does not mean that Nehemiah or Jeremiah carried out their leadership without God's Spirit! Equally, people may be excellent Christian leaders without ever appreciating or expressing their dependence on God's Spirit for their leadership. The Holy Spirit's task is not to draw attention to himself anyway. So we need not doubt our Christian leaders or our leadership simply because they, or we, do not speak about it in a particular way. Equally, using correct jargon does not guarantee the best leadership. Clearly the issues are deeper than this. We need to consider the biblical material about the gifts of the Spirit and see how they can enhance leadership.

The Gifts of the Spirit in the Bible

A glance at the four most important passages on spiritual gifts in the New Testament makes some things clear. Spiritual gifts are given not for us to boast about, or quarrel about, or be jealous about. Nor are they given for us to admire. They are given to equip the whole Church to carry out its God-given task of evangelizing and serving the world. Christ gives gifts through the Holy Spirit "...to prepare all God's people for the work of Christian service..." (Ephesians 4.12).

Although this verse can be taken to refer to the special leadership gifts of apostles, prophets, evangelists, pastors, and teachers, there are two reasons why we need to be aware of the whole range of gifts which the Holy Spirit makes available. First, we need to find out which gifts are relevant for our leadership. Secondly, we need to know what gifts might help others be a more effective part of the whole. In the next chapter we shall find how we can identify our gifts and in Chapter 7 how we can work best together.

Now let us try to get a clear grasp of the gifts which are mentioned in the New Testament. First, we will compile a list. On page 69 is a diagram on which the twenty-eight gifts of the Spirit mentioned in the New Testament can be noted. It is helpful to read the passages and compile the complete list.

Next we need a brief description of each of them. Such descriptions differ according to the authors but the following is a basic and clear description of the gifts based on one of the best known authors on spiritual gifts and church growth (in brackets is the *Good News Bible* equivalent).

Prophecy — (the gift of speaking God's message) the ability to receive and communicate an immediate message of God to his people through a divinely anointed utterance.

Service — the ability to identify the unmet needs involved in a task related to God's work, and to make use of available resources to meet those needs and help accomplish the desired goals.

Teaching — the ability to communicate information relevant to the health and ministry of the body and its members in such a way that others will learn.

Exhortation — (encouragement) the ability to minister words of comfort, consolation, encouragement, and counsel to other members of the body in such a way that they feel helped and healed.

Giving — (sharing) the ability to contribute material resources to the work of the Lord with liberality and cheerfulness.

How many can you identify?
Please look up the passage and fill in the "parcels"
Romans 12.3–8; 1 Corinthians 12.4–11, 27–30; Ephesians 3.7; 4.11–12; 1 Peter 4.10–11; Acts 16.16–18; 1 Corinthians 7.7; 1 Timothy 2.1.

Leadership — (authority) the ability to set goals in accordance with God's purpose for the future and to communicate these goals to others in such a way that they voluntarily and harmoniously work together to accomplish those goals for the glory of God.
Mercy — (shows kindness) the ability to feel genuine empathy and compassion for individuals, both Christian and non-Christian, who suffer distressing physical, mental, or emotional problems, and to translate that compassion into cheerfully done deeds that reflect Christ's love and alleviate the suffering.
Wisdom — the ability to know the mind of the Holy Spirit in such a way as to receive insight into how given knowledge may best be applied to specific needs arising in the body of Christ.
Knowledge — the ability to discover, collect, analyze and clarify information and ideas that are pertinent to the growth and well-being of the body of Christ.
Faith — the ability to discern with extraordinary confidence the will and purposes of God for the future of his work.
Healings — the ability to serve as human intermediaries through whom it pleases God to cure and restore, apart from the use of natural means.
Miracles — the ability to serve as human intermediaries through whom it pleases God to perform acts that are perceived by observers to have altered the ordinary course of nature.
Discerning of spirits — (the ability to tell the difference between gifts that come from the Spirit and those that do not) the ability to know with assurance whether certain behaviour purported to be of God is in reality divine, human, or satanic.
Tongues — (to speak in strange tongues) the ability to speak to God in a language you have never learned. (This is generally the major ministry through the gift of tongues.) To receive and communicate an immediate message of God to his people through a divinely anointed utterance in a language you have never learned. To use in certain situations a known language, having never learned it, to communicate God's message.
Interpretation of tongues — (explaining what is said) the ability to make known in the vernacular the message of one who speaks in tongues.
Apostle — the ability to assume and exercise general leadership with an extraordinary authority in spiritual matters that is spontaneously recognized and appreciated.
Helps — the ability to invest the talents they have in the life and ministry of other members of the body, thus enabling the person

helped to increase the effectiveness of his or her spiritual gifts.
Administration — (direct others) the ability to understand clearly the immediate and long-range goals of a particular unit of the body of Christ and to devise and execute effective plans for the accomplishment of these goals.
Voluntary poverty — (giving away everything) the ability to renounce material comforts and luxury and adopt a personal life style equivalent to those living at the poverty level in a given society in order to serve God more effectively.
Martyrdom — (giving up the body to be burned) the ability to undergo suffering for the faith even to death while consistently displaying a joyous and victorious attitude that brings glory to God.
Evangelist — the ability to share the gospel with unbelievers in such a way that men and women become Jesus' disciples and responsible members of the body of Christ.
Pastor — the ability to assume a long-term personal responsibility for the spiritual welfare of a group of believers.
Hospitality — (opening homes to others) the ability to provide an open house and a warm welcome for those in need of food and lodging.
Exorcism — (sending evil spirits out of people) the ability to cast out demons and evil spirits.
Celibacy — (living alone) the ability to remain single and enjoy it; to be unmarried and not suffer undue sexual temptations.
Missionary — (a servant of the gospel) the ability to minister whatever spiritual gifts they have in a second culture.
Intercession — (prayers for people) the ability to pray for extended periods of time on a regular basis and see frequent and specific answer to their prayers to a degree much greater than that which is expected of the average Christian.

Of course, it is possible to give a great deal more detail on all of these gifts. Any of the following books will help if the reader wishes to investigate the gifts more closely.

General

Arnold Bittlinger, *Gifts and Graces* (Hodder and Stoughton, 1967).
Arnold Bittlinger, *Gifts and Ministries* (Hodder and Stoughton, 1974).
E Gibbs, *I Believe in Church Growth* (Hodder and Stoughton,

1981) pp.319–356.
David Pytches, *Come Holy Spirit* (Hodder and Stoughton, 1985), pp.57–127.
C P Wagner, *Your Spiritual Gifts Can Help Your Church Grow* (Marc Europe, 1985).

Gifts with a Leadership Bias

P Greenslade, *Leadership* (Marshalls Paperbacks, 1984), especially pp.131–197.
C Sibthorpe, *A Man Under Authority* (Kingsway, 1984).

Specific Gifts

Leadership — C P Wagner, *Leading Your Church to Growth* (Marc, 1984).
Discernment — Douglas McBain, *Eyes That See* (Marshall Pickering, 1986).
Listening gifts — J Huggett, *Listening to God* (Hodder and Stoughton, 1986).
Prophecy — W Gruden, *The Gift of Prophecy* (Kingsway Publications, 1988) and T Pain, *Prophecy* (Kingsway Publications, 1986).
Tongues etc. — T Pain, *Tongues and Explanations* (Kingsway Publications, 1986).
Teaching — R B Zuch, *The Holy Spirit in Your Teaching* (Victor Books, SP Publications, 1984).
Intercession — T Pain, *Intercession* (Kingsway Publications, 1986) and Margaret Magdalen, *Jesus — Man of Prayer* (Hodder and Stoughton, 1987),

We shall consider certain gifts in more detail as we investigate a few of the many issues which the matter of spiritual gifts raises.

The Problem with Gifts...

Is the Composite List Inclusive or Exclusive?

In other words, once we have listed and understood all twenty-eight gifts do we know all the gifts which God does, or can, give to people? Or can we expect or accept that other gifts can be gifts of the Spirit? My own view is that the gift list is not exclusive. There are other gifts which come from the Spirit.

There are several reasons why I believe this. First, the lists are so varied in length and character that their nature does not suggest they are meant to be comprehensive. Secondly, the contexts do not indicate that they are meant to be all inclusive. Thirdly, the way some gifts are mentioned in isolation also suggests there could well be other "stray" gifts. Perhaps, most importantly and practically, some of the gifts seem so general that they could incorporate all manner of more specific gifts, for instance the "helps" of Romans 12.

Are all the Gifts Available Today?

Many commentators and writers used to argue that the supernatural gifts ceased with the death of the final apostle and the provision of Scripture, making the authentification of miracles no longer necessary, for instance. Again I find this position personally unacceptable (E Gibbs, *I Believe in Church Growth,* p.321). I do not think the scriptures used support this position, nor can I dismiss the contemporary evidence for the existence of the supernatural gifts such as miracles, tongues, words of knowledge etc. However, for those who believe that the supernatural gifts ceased with the apostles, the rest of the gifts are still an important issue for the leadership of the Church; although it must be recognized that some of what I will be saying needs to be modified if this "cessationist" view is maintained.[2]

What is the Relationship Between Natural and Spiritual Gifts?

This question uses the word natural in a somewhat different way to the previous question. A person might have the natural ability for teaching prior to conversion or, as another example, be a good administrator. When they are converted and are born of the Spirit does that mean that they automatically have the spiritual gift of teaching or administration? My answer would be no. The person can teach without it being a spiritual gift. If the natural gift is shadowed (over-shadowed) by a corresponding spiritual gift then it will produce a spiritually powerful effect (E Gibbs, *I Believe in Church Growth,* p.328). Natural gifts should not be despised but neither should they be substituted for spiritual gifts. Equally, someone who, prior to conversion, had no apparent aptitude for teaching or administration, could receive the spiritual gifts of teaching or administration.

An even more complex and contentious issue concerns natural

"supernatural" gifts such as clairvoyance. I believe that some people have such gifts. These people do not automatically develop equivalent spiritual gifts when they become Christians. Just as a teacher can go on teaching without it being a spiritual gift, so someone can use their clairvoyant natural gift without it becoming prophecy or words of knowledge. Indeed I would argue that it is vital for such a gift to be renounced so that the Spirit has free access to give gifts as he chooses.

Are Spiritual Gifts Permanent Endowments or Temporary Enablings?

Put another way, is the gift given to meet a situation or is it given to a person? It seems to me that the answer is probably both. For instance, people who are regularly involved in a healing ministry experience, when faced with specific needs, bursts of power to heal. People who have words of knowledge sometimes seem to have them almost at will, sometimes just occasionally. Someone who has a gift may find the effectiveness of the gift is seriously affected by the quality of their relationship with God, even though it is true they are not "rewards for devotion or service" (E Gibbs, *I Believe in Church Growth,* p.324).

When gifts become a permanent enabling of the person then they lead on to ministries. For instance, a person who frequently exercises a gift of prophecy is likely to become a prophet. A person who frequently exercises the gift of leadership is likely to become a leader and so on.[3] Hence, we should not imagine that a person who has a specific gift only has that gift, or can always exercise that gift, more than anyone else, or that someone else cannot manifest that gift. We should never forget the sovereignty of the Spirit. "...the same Spirit... as he wishes, he gives a different gift to each person." (1 Corinthians 12.11)

As they are Gifts can we do Anything to Obtain Them or Develop Them?

In fact, if we do strive so to do are we not being arrogant, disobedient or, at best, betraying our ignorance of the fact that they are gifts? I believe that being gifts emphasizes that we cannot deserve them. Paul and Peter emphasize we need to use our gifts properly, surely implying that we can misuse or under use the gifts. Practical experience indicates that with use, supported by spiritual resources of prayer and encouragement, gifts will grow stronger and more effective with use, just as normal gifts will. However, I do sense that overexposure and demands which are too strong can reduce effectiveness too. In the next chapter I will indicate how gifts can be acquired — some will prefer to think of them as already potentially present. I do not wish to argue about this as it makes no practical difference. We are still encouraged in Scripture to seek for gifts! The matter of spiritual gifts is so vital for leadership in the Church that it cannot be neglected even if some points are contentious. We must now focus our attention on the specific issue of leadership and spiritual gifts.

Leadership and Spiritual Gifts

We need to be careful not to get mentally sidetracked and so now we focus clearly on the issue of spiritual gifts and leadership. To help us we can ask the question "Which of all these spiritual gifts are gifts for leaders?"

Most people are clear that in the light of Ephesians 4 the top level of leadership gifts are apostles, prophets, evangelists and pastors and teachers.[4] Some would argue that the first two ceased at the end of the apostolic era, others that a modern equivalent is still vitally necessary. Eddie Gibbs is helpful here. He shows us that the apostle's ministry was to ensure the validity of the Church's message and to promote Christian expansion on a transcongregational basis. He argues that a similar ministry is needed today. People who are free to roam, who have a pioneering spirit, who are more concerned with tomorrow than yesterday. The prophet also has a transcongregational ministry.

On the other hand, and in contrast to much of our experience, the evangelist was located in the local congregation. So was the pastor-teacher, although there were also visiting pastor-teachers.[5] The New Testament recognizes other local ministers — bishops, elders, and deacons. These, unlike the above five, are not specified as gifts! They, too, seem to be specifically related to the local congregation. Any survey of the New Testament shows clearly that there was a rich variety in the leadership gifts and ministries of the early church.

> *In the midst of all this confusing variety, one thing stands out clearly, namely that there was a plurality of leadership in the local church. Furthermore, the leadership ministries did not*

> *displace the charismata* (spiritual gifts) *distributed throughout the membership.*[6]

Furthermore, gifts and ministries were not to be rejected by the local congregation because they, from the perception of that congregation, were temporary. That is, they were transcongregational.

We need to see clearly that in Ephesians 4 the gifts of Christ become people with those gifts, who have ministries. In some cases, as with prophecy/prophet, the spiritual gift is verbally tied to the person. In other cases, such as apostle, this is not so, that is there is no mention of a specific "apostleship" gift or even "pastorship" gift. Was there a specific "bishop" gift, or "deaconship" gift? Well, for deacons we are told the original qualifications, and it wasn't deaconship! (see Acts 6.3, 5) We must also admit we don't know for sure whether a prophet only needed to exercise the gift of prophecy regularly to become a prophet, or did he need to be "full of the Holy Spirit" etc. as well?

Further, just as the deacon needs wisdom, so other gifts are valuable for different kinds of leadership and different situations. Any gift can make a contribution and modulate the style of leadership, and any situation can benefit from a particular gift mix. Therefore, every spiritual gift can be integrated into the leader's equipping. We shall consider this more in the next chapter.

There is another reason why all the spiritual gifts are relevant to each leader. Every person in the Church, and each gift, has a contribution to make to the effective mission of the Church. Leaders have the task of utilizing and orchestrating people and their gifts to this end. So the leader needs to understand not only each gift, but also to know how to develop and make effective each gift. Again an issue we shall consider later.

Before this, however, it is worth approaching the issue of leadership and gifts from a different angle. If any group is to function well, that is to be able to achieve its aims, there are four dimensions to the leadership it requires: they are thinking, deciding, people, and tasks. This can be illustrated on the diagram opposite.

Any group with responsibilities and aims, whether these are overtly stated or presumed, needs leadership in all four of these dimensions. If the thinking is not carried out, time will be wasted because the wrong policies and procedures might be adopted and inadequate planning could create hold-ups, leading to frustration and a sense of failure. If the group enjoys thinking so much it

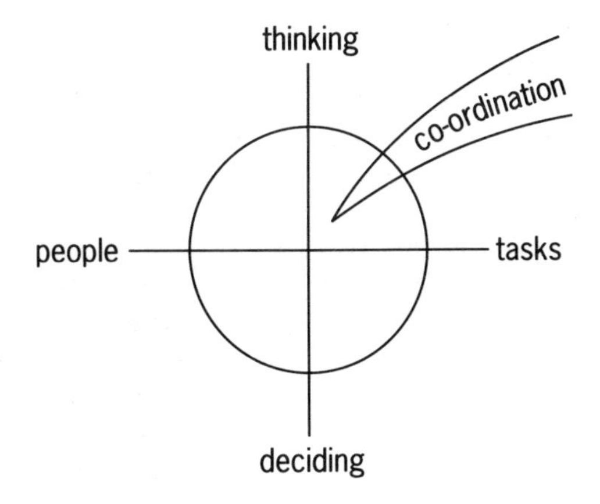

never decides anything, or even uses the "talk shop" as an excuse for inaction, the group won't achieve very much. If people are not affirmed and helped to relate, then there will be lack of motivation and internal friction, which will overlay and intertwine the thinking and the doing. If the tasks are not carried out because no-one wants to upset anyone, then again nothing will be accomplished.

The balance between these four aspects of a group will vary according to its *raison d'être.* Clearly a group concerned with the fabric of the church will need to decide more, whilst a group concerned with the financial policy of the church will need to think more, whilst a group for sharing problems will need to be people orientated, whilst a group handling the education of the church will be task orientated. But each of these groups need leadership in all four dimensions. The balance will also be affected by the individual. Some people need a lot more help than others etc. But leadership is not only concerned with the four dimensions, but the co-ordination of them. This needs distinctive skills too. Of course, any one leader need not personally supply the leadership but they must ensure it is happening appropriately.

Many of the gifts listed and explained on pp.68–71 can be plotted on the diagram used as axes of a graph. For instance teaching goes somewhere in the thinking/tasks quadrant, encouraging is in the thinking/people quadrant, kindness in the people/acting quadrant.

It is helpful to go through the gifts and allocate them to a quadrant or to the co-ordination function. Then, if we become aware that our group could function better with help in one or two dimensions, we will be able to see the kind of gifts which should help improve the health of the group.

In the next chapter we shall see more clearly how the insights we are gaining about spiritual gifts can make a practical difference to us as leaders, to those who lead us, to the fulfilment of the Church's God given tasks and to the growth of the kingdom.

Tasks

○ × 1. Describe a situation and consider which gifts the leader used. Which gifts would have helped the leader? Which people and gifts were a gift to the leader?

○ × 2. List the New Testament gifts and ask around the group for two illustrations of how and when they might be useful for the leader.

○ × 3. Compile some New Testament illustrations of gifts being used in leadership functions. Think of contemporary situations where the same gifts would be helpful. e.g. Acts 16.1–40 Timothy was a gift to Paul. Paul exercised authority/apostleship by delivering rules and word of wisdom (verses 6–10 etc.).

○ × 4. Allocate the New Testament gifts to the four quadrants. Discuss your presentation with others in your group.

△ 5. Talk with your prayer partners about the gift of prayer. How you can help each other, how your faith is growing, how the Holy Spirit helps you to pray, how God is answering your prayers and how prayer is helping you.

References — Chapter 5

1. C P Wagner *Leading Your Church to Growth* (Marc, 1984), p.131, 132.
2. Cf. P Masters *The Healing Epidemic* (Wakeman, 1980), pp.112–135 especially p.132. "The charismata… which have an ongoing place in the life of the church are… the teaching, pastoring and leading ministries of the church…"
3. Cf. for instance, A Bittlinger, *Gifts and Ministries* (Hodder and Stoughton, 1974), pp.26–27.
4. Cf. A Bittlinger, op.cit. pp.52–99.
   E Gibbs, *I Believe in Church Growth* (Hodder and Stoughton, 1981), pp.340–356.
   P Greenslade, *Leadership* (Marshalls Paperbacks, 1984), pp.136–172.

5. A Bittlinger, op.cit. pp.29–51.
   Greenslade, op.cit. pp.183–197.
6. E Gibbs, op.cit. p.345.

CHAPTER 6

GROWING GIFTS FOR GROWING LEADERS

"Unidentified gifts represent unlived life"[1]

Goal

To understand the gifts of the Spirit and then increase our leadership effectiveness through discovering and using them.

Aims

1. To help us value our gifts and other people's too.
2. To provide further resources for doing this more adequately.
3. To understand how the gifts we have modulate the way we lead most effectively.
4. To recognize that other people have gifts, and this has implications for leaders i.e. teams.
5. To see how we can develop the gifts we have.
6. To see how we can receive new gifts from the Spirit.

Main Scriptures

Romans 12.3–8; 1 Corinthians 12—4; Ephesians 4; 1 Peter 4.11–12.

Introduction

Someone I know always calls antique shops junk shops! When some people look in the window they see goods which are old, and often marked or damaged. The goods are often not arranged artistically, and there are no glossy packages. Old things do not appeal to my friend; but one person's junk can be another person's treasure, because they collect or use the items. The *Antiques Road Show* demonstrates that many of us do have items of considerable worth stored around our homes. When a piece of pottery is valued in hundreds of pounds, or a battered table proves to be worth thousands of pounds because of the craftsman who made it, then there is a look of surprise and delight on the owner's face. The owners don't seem to mind that their own evaluation was wrong. Their heirloom has been understood and affirmed in public, and their financial prospects improved.

Scripture tells us that God has given gifts to every member of his Church. This divine "craftsman" gives worth to everyone. Many of us have never properly appreciated the gifts of God's Spirit in us. Sometimes we have not understood what the gift was and have used it for the wrong purpose. Or, having lived with the gift for so long, we do not value it fully. Again, like an old painting whose fineness and colour have faded with age and grime, our gifts have dulled. Sometimes we do not know we have the gift in the cupboard at all!

What a Gift I am!

We often fail to appreciate the full value of our spiritual gifts because we mentally disregard who their maker is. Paul stresses that we should not despise any gift which comes from God's Spirit. "There are different kinds of spiritual gifts but the same Spirit gives them." (1 Corinthians 12.4).

Chapters 12 – 14 of 1 Corinthians show that a particular congregation could overvalue some gifts and neglect or despise others. Paul's point is that a healthy church needs to recognize the contribution that each gift makes to the health and proper functioning of the church. So Paul writes to promote a proper use and appreciation of the whole range of the gifts from God.

In the last chapter we saw that certain spiritual gifts are recognized most clearly in the Bible as leadership gifts — apostles, prophets, evangelists, pastors, teachers etc. But we also saw that such gifts are people, rather than abilities people have. (Although, of course, such people need appropriate gifts.) Such gifts are highly desirable for particular levels in the life of the Church. Other gifts are also significant for leadership. What is vital is that we can honestly recognize the gifts we have from God so that our kind of leadership can be appropriate to the particular gifts, and the particular mix of gifts, that God has given. Of equal, if not greater, importance is our need to recognize what gifts God has not given us, so that we do not try to lead in areas of the Church's life for which we are not equipped.

In Britain our natural tendency is to want to avoid leadership and to minimize the awareness of our gifts, and the projection of that awareness to others. Nowhere has this tendency been stronger than in the churches. Many subtle, and not so subtle, forces have been at work which inhibit an honest assessment of our gifts and make us reluctant to make those gifts available for God's Church, and particularly for proper leadership in the Church. It is as though the only gifts we can own are modesty and caution! Caution, because if we offer to lead we might not be good enough to succeed, and failure is the one thing above all others we cannot live with in the Church! Modesty, because it is clearly wrong to be proud. It is not hard to perceive such attitudes are not entirely biblical ("Who do I think I am daring to write this book" I ask myself!).

We need help, then, to come to terms with the scriptural truths. According to Jesus it is wrong to bury our God-given talents. Modesty needs to be replaced with honesty. The honesty to accept the generosity of God who gives gifts lavishly to his people. Caution needs to be replaced with creativity which is willing to experiment with the most effective ways of using our gifts, and the gifts of others, in the leadership of his Church. Before we can be bold and creative we need to recognize our gifts, remembering always who the master craftsman is.[2]

There are many ways in which we can come to discover the spiritual gifts we have. The simplest is rather like the bird watcher. We carry our bird book with us and compare what we see with the account in the book. When we have enough details to assure us that we have made a correct identification then we can read everything else about the bird — where it comes from, what kind of nest it builds, what food it eats, its average wing span, its rarity value and so on. Identification leads us to a greater understanding and appreciation.

Which Gifts?

It is well worth pausing now and returning to the list of gifts with the brief description and definition provided for each gift on pages 68-71. Probably as you read through that list you thought "Yes I think James or Ann has that gift" or even "So that's what I've got", "I wonder if the way I respond in such and such a situation means God has given me that gift?" Try and recall again the gifts you thought you had or might have had. Also write down the names of people you think have specific gifts. I suggest we use three categories only for each gift. (Place other people who come to mind in a column at the far end.)

fts	Yes	No	Possibly	Others
peak God's message				
ervice				
eaching etc.				

As you do this it is worth noting how you felt. Did you find it easier when you could tick the "No" column than when you ticked the "Yes"? Was it exciting or frightening when you ticked "possibly" (maybe you even felt vaguely guilty in being so presumptuous). I personally hope that when you placed a tick you felt good, whether it was a "yes" or "no" or "possibly", but few of us do feel like that. It isn't our fault and it isn't disastrous. God has provided us with ways of growing in our ability to be comfortable with the gifts he is giving to us. I wonder, too, whether you found it easier to recognize gifts in others than in yourself? Most of us do. What reasons are there for this?

In terms of discovering our spiritual gifts the bird identification has a few problems. One is that, so to speak, we are often looking not at a fully developed bird but a fledgling. As we try and see what gifts God has given us we are looking at potential rather than perfection. Another difficulty we have is that to the novice one bird can look like several other species. Indeed, as I look at the pictures in the bird book whole groups of birds can look so alike I despair that I shall ever be able to differentiate them. This point is not quite so devastating as we might think. Often those birds whose appearances are similar are related to one another. So, if we can't differentiate in our mind between words of wisdom, knowledge or exhortation, let alone decide which spiritual gift God has given us, we might at least know the kind of work for which God has equipped us. Perhaps our greatest disadvantage is that we are not looking outwards, we are essentially looking inwards. At least this is how it seems when we are honestly trying to assess the gifts God has given to us personally.

For this reason, if for no other, it is worth approaching our gifts somewhat more indirectly. A well-known and well-tried method is that developed by the Rev L Misselbrook. We shall consider how best to use this in a moment but first work through the list below as indicated. Perhaps it is helpful to pray now. If these words help then please use them:

Dear Father, Thank you that Jesus teaches us you are a generous and kind God. Thank you for all the gifts I see in others which I enjoy and from which I gain so much. Thank you that as a Christian the Holy Spirit lives in me and has given me gifts.

I confess I don't find it easy to admit this or to be sure what gifts I have. Help me now to be relaxed and accept myself as you have made me. Help me to discover and confirm the gifts the Holy Spirit has given me. Thank you, through Jesus Christ. Amen

Personal Assessment

Now read the following statements and mark yourself out of 5 for each.

If you give yourself 5 it will be one of your very strong points.

If you give yourself 0 or 1 it will be one of your very weak points.

If you give yourself 2 or 3 it will be an average point.

1. I am good at listening
2. I enjoy explaining things to others from the Bible
3. I love preaching or talking about Jesus to a congregation or group

4. I am often used to bring others to Christ
5. I enjoy administrative work
6. I feel a deep, caring love for those who are ill and a call to help them get well
7. I am handy at most things and adaptable
8. I am deeply concerned about the world and social affairs
9. I am usually looked to for a lead
10. I make helpful relationships with others easily
11. Others are helped when I teach them things
12. I love the study and work in preparing a message
13. God has given me a great love for others and a longing to win them for him
14. I can organize well, clearly, and efficiently
15. Others find my presence soothing and healing
16. I like helping other people
17. I am active in service in the community
18. In a group I am often elected chairman or leader
19. I can encourage others and help bear burdens
20. I love study and finding the facts
21. My sermons have been clearly blessed to others
22. I find my life is full of opportunities to witness to Christ
23. I love doing office work and do it thoroughly
24. I have sometimes laid hands on the sick and they have been healed
25. I am a practical type
26. I am very aware of the needs of society today and feel called to do something about it
27. When leading something I put a lot of preparation into it
28. I really care about other people
29. I have patience in helping others understand Christian things
30. I feel a clear call to preach
31. I love to talk to others about Jesus
32. I am painstaking about details in organisation
33. I spend time praying with and for sick people
34. I spend much time helping others in practical ways
35. I feel God is at work in the world today and I must work along with him there
36. I am good at delegating work to others in a team setting

Next transfer the scores you have given yourself for each statement to the **Gift Grid** by putting your score in the appropriate box.

Then add up the totals across and enter them in the final column.

Gift Grid Totals

1	10	19	28	A
2	11	20	29	B
3	12	21	30	C
4	13	22	31	D
5	14	23	32	E
6	15	24	33	F
7	16	25	34	G
8	17	26	35	H
9	18	27	36	I

Interpretation

If the highest total is in column A the gift is pastoral
If the highest total is in column B the gift is teaching
If the highest total is in column C the gift is preaching
If the highest total is in column D the gift is evangelism
If the highest total is in column E the gift is administration
If the highest total is in column F the gift is healing
If the highest total is in column G the gift is practical help
If the highest total is in column H the gift is service to society
If the highest total is in column I the gift is leadership

The Gift Grid as a Transferable Tool

The value of the Gift Grid is that it is easily transferable.[3] How and why does this help? First, we can transfer the grid by getting other people who know us well to do it for us. Simply by changing the "I am good at listening" to "David (or he/she) is good at listening" others can provide us with their perception on the gifts God has given to us. This has several advantages. One is that it removes our susceptibility to self-doubt about our own observations, and provides a degree of objectivity. Sometimes it will remove our false notions about our ability! People's lack of feedback may have prevented us from distinguishing fact from fantasy. Often it will confirm our perceptions. Sometimes it will point us to gifts we didn't know we had. A group of ornithologists are less likely to make a wrong observation than one on his own. Another is that those who help us see our gifts can also contribute to their development and employment.

The second way in which we can transfer the grid is that we can use it to help other people find their gifts. As leaders we need all the gifts God is giving to others if our group is going to do God's work fully. So we need other people to own and use their gifts. This is a fairly comfortable way for people to do this. Then they can use it to help others, and so on. Because it is simple and cheap it can be used widely and effectively.

The third way in which the grid is transferable is that it is easily adaptable. For instance, we might find people had difficulty in handling a 0–5 scoring system so we could print columns to tick: Yes, No, Possible. We could then give numerical values 2, 0, 1, and amend the grid and interpretation accordingly. We can adjust and amplify the accounts to suit our culture and congregation. Eddie Gibbs shows how this can be done.[4] For instance, his account of the healing gift is:

> *I have a desire to pray for the sick. Sometimes, I have wanted to reach out and touch the person as I prayed. Afterwards, a number of people have made a remarkable recovery, often beyond reasonable medical expectation.*[5]

Further, we can use this approach to discern gifts which are not covered by Misselbrook. Eddie Gibbs says "Sometimes my prayers have resulted in an incredible occurrence or chain of circumstances". I wonder if you can work out to which gift this relates?[6] All this makes the approach a useful tool to help us and others identify their gifts.[7]

Further Reflections

This approach to gift discovery tells us more about what kind of gift we are meant to be to the Church than the kind of gifts we have. It is functional, but this is a helpful bias for a book like ours which is concerned about improving practical outcomes and church growth. If we look at the gift accounts they relate not only to results — what happens when the gift is exercised, but also to felt responses — what the person using the gift feels to the use of the gift (and by implication what they feel when they have to do a task for which they are not gifted!).

Both these features are indicators of whether we have a gift or not. The results only help if we already use that gift. By the time the results are out it may not seem all that helpful to be able to give the gift a biblical name. Yet there are still values. First, it helps everyone recognize that a gift is no less a gift, and no less a spiritual gift because, for instance, it is practical. This has many important repercussions for the individual and the fellowship in terms of affirmation, harmony, and balance. Secondly, giving the gift a name may help us see how that gift (rather then the functions which result from it) can be utilized in other situations. The felt responses may be an important clue to identify spiritual gifts which have not been developed and deployed. Whilst such felt responses need ultimately to be confirmed by practical results we need to be cautious about squashing giftings. It is true here, even more than in horticulture, that big trees from little acorns grow. One of the necessary skills of leaders is to foster the growth of gifts that the Holy Spirit has planted.

As we involve others in evaluating us it helps them accept the value of finding out the gifts God gives for themselves, and for the church generally. Thus, it prepares the soil of the Church. But when we first invite people to assess us it can seem a risky business. They might say we don't have this gift on which we pride ourselves. Worse still they might discover we are not omnicompetent!

A Risky Business?

Identifying gifts, especially our gifts as leaders, can feel a very dubious business and can make us feel very vulnerable. As we invite other people to let us know what gifts we have and don't have we can feel extremely exposed. They might realize that we're not very competent to chair the meetings, or mend the fuses, or keep the filing system (what system?) up to date. The trouble is compounded if they expect us to do these things. (We shall consider the issue of expectations more fully in Chapter 8 on Limitations to Leading). The inevitable conclusion is that we feel "I am no good for the job". We also feel we shall lose respect etc.

These fears are real enough and need to be recognized and accepted in ourselves and others. But the fears are rarely justified and there are many advantages in coming to terms with ourselves. Theologically put, no-one, not even the Archbishop of Canterbury, has been given all the gifts, so no-one is meant by God to do everything. If God does not hold us responsible for doing everything who can be against us! Realizing this can be very releasing — but the process of realizing and releasing is often difficult and painful.

Let's consider this at a more practical level. We are part of the body of Christ and we do have gifts. We don't have to be omnicompetent leaders because God doesn't want it. If we use the gifts God has given us as much as possible we are likely to be more effective, to enjoy life more and to have more energy for doing more. If we minimize the time spent on tasks we are not gifted for we shall make room for other people to use their God-given gifts. In other words, recognizing the gifts we lack helps us realize what kinds of people we need with us. This frees us to affirm them, to value them, and employ them more effectively for the kingdom. We are much freer to see other people as partners, rather than pressures, in the kingdom of God. It also helps other people, both to see we are not omnicompetent and to understand we don't see ourselves that way either. They will feel more needed and, more importantly, will feel they don't need to be omnicompetent before we can use them or they can offer to be used.

I used to feel far more guilty than I do now about getting other people to do the things I didn't enjoy doing because I wasn't gifted for them. The great release is to discover others can enjoy doing what you hate and they would hate to have to do what you enjoy. Everyone can be happier if they are maximizing the use of their gifts and maximize the appreciation of other people's.

An additional benefit is that, eventually, people will no longer expect us to be good at the things for which we are not gifted. We may still have to do some of these things but, if we can honestly say "It's not my gift", they tend to be more supportive and will be able to compensate for our weaknesses.

We may see opportunities which need seizing and perceive the gifts which are needed and know we don't have the right gifts. It may be that the opportunity is not for us or our church. But it may be that it is not so much an opportunity as a necessity. Doesn't the gift analysis paralyze us? I don't believe so, for two reasons. First, we can pray for God to provide the gifts we need in the people we already have. Secondly, we can pray for him to provide us with new people with the gifts we require. So gift analysis helps to sharpen our prayer focus, and I can testify to some interesting answers to such prayers. (Hint — If you don't have people with the gift of prayer faith, discover them. Perhaps they are your prayer partners, share with them the needs you see for gifting, and get them praying. You don't have to have all the gifts!)

For leaders, especially central leaders, our fear can be that we don't have the right leadership gifts and therefore we are not meant to lead. My fundamental belief is that what gifts we have might affect the way we lead, they might even affect where we lead, but it is most unlikely to affect whether we lead.[8] The more probable outcome is that we shall learn to lead in ways appropriate to our gifts, involve others in that process and find that we are free to be the kind of leaders God wants us to be. But let me emphasize again to all concerned that such realization is never cheap and the application of it costly. The higher up the leadership hierarchy you go, the greater the price. So please understand, pray for and support leaders as they move through this process. We all need people who will not only work with us but love us if we are to grow in this kind of way.

How we Lead

Recently I heard a taped message explaining how the eight gifts mentioned in Romans would affect the way eight Christians, with those gifts, might make a hospital visit. Each of the eight could visit, each could make a positive contribution but each would be distinct. For instance, the teacher would have done research on the illness and be able to explain all about it to the patient in such a way that the patient understood. The person with the gift of encouragement would refer to people they had known with the same problem and how they had got better and were leading normal lives. The person with the gift of serving would bring in tissues and offer to wash the clothes. The person with the gift of generosity would bring grapes and flowers and glossy magazines etc. Each could visit effectively and (as long as they didn't all come at once!) together would make a tremendous visiting team.

In the same way I am convinced we can all lead, but our way of leading will be different. It is, in fact, important to know what are our main spiritual gifts because they may well indicate the kind of leadership style which will "normally" be most appropriate for us to use. On page 56 we used a leadership style spectrum. We can now superimpose spiritual gifts on this spectrum as indicated in tables 4 and 5.

If our gifts are all on the right hand side we would find it difficult to operate at the authoritarian end. If our gifts were all at the left hand end we would find it hard to operate at the permissive end, and probably even the democratic. If all our gifts were central we would probably find it difficult to operate at either end, and the democratic style would seem to us the normal Christian one. If we have gifts from different sections of the spectrum then we will have the strength of being able to operate comfortably across the spectrum but the disadvantage that our leadership may appear erratic, and so on.

These insights help us to realize several things. If a task requires authoritarian leadership and our gifts are to the right perhaps we would lead best by offering to babysit (kindness) and release someone else with more appropriate gifts for this kind of leadership. Or we might share the leadership with another and use our gift to encourage and support others in the group when they feel hurt by the dynamics of an authoritarian leader. For, as we have seen, some tasks and situations are best handled with one kind of leadership and some with another. These insights will also help us appreciate why we find someone else's style strange, or even offensive: their gifts are different and so their appropriate leadership style is different. However, what Paul says about gifts also applies to kinds of leadership. Don't despise what God has chosen and given to another. Learn to work harmoniously with others. We should also try to operate over an expanding range of leadership styles and one way to help in this is to pray for spiritual gifts from a different part of the spectrum.

Table 4 Spiritual gifts and leadership

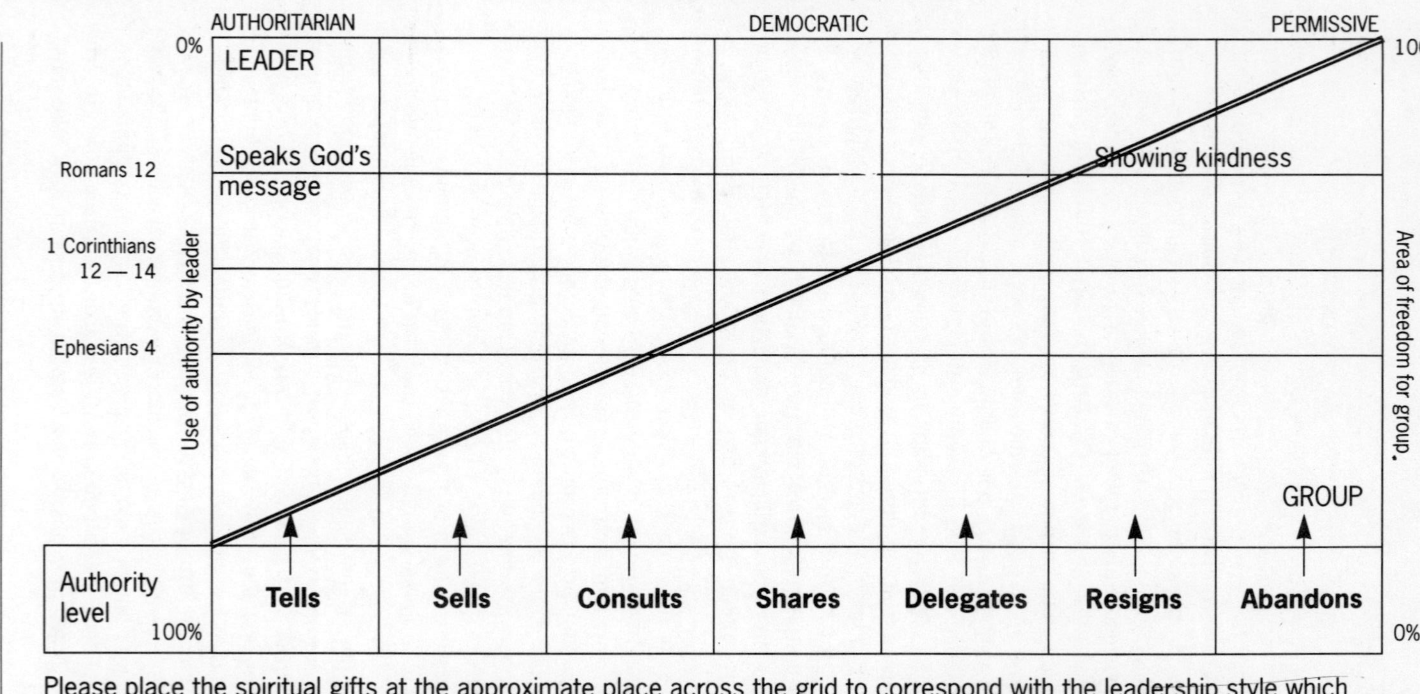

Please place the spiritual gifts at the approximate place across the grid to correspond with the leadership style which would result with that gift in operation e.g. speaks God's message — authoritarian, showing kindness (makes no demands) — permissive. My assessment is on table 5.

Table 5 **Spiritual gifts and leadership**

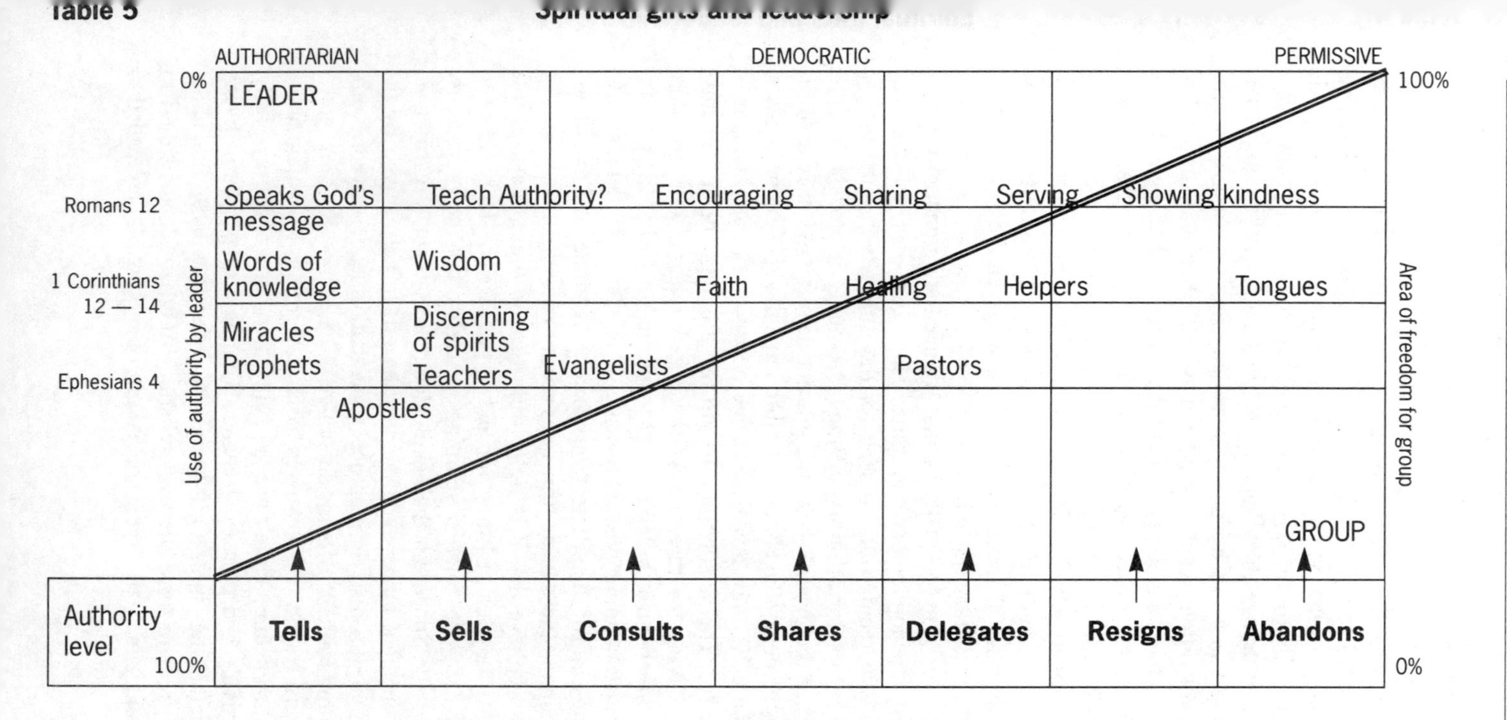

We may place the gifts in different positions because of different understandings and experiences. Above is my position for those gifts most relevant to leadership.

New Gifts?

I believe it is right for us to seek new spiritual gifts. Paul says "...Set your hearts on spiritual gifts..." 1 Corinthians 14.1 (please note Paul uses the plural verb not the singular), and we are to do this especially for the ones which build up the body of Christ. It is somewhat strange that Wagner apparently contradicts this. "It is not up to you as a Christian to place an order for the gift or gifts which you might want".[9] Whilst it is important and scriptual to recognize the sovereignty of God it is surely just as right to seek for gifts as it is to seek for healing. Of course there must be safeguards. We don't seek for gifts for our own advantage or to establish our superiority. We do seek them so the body can function as God wants. Wagner is right to say "our first responsibility is to discover our gifts".[10] It may be that God has given the gifts we need to us or to others in our fellowship.

However, it may equally be that we need additional gifts or we need to develop embryonic gifts. How best can we do this? Normally it seems right to seek for the gifts which our situation demands, not for arbitrary giftings. Normally it is right that the church, or the group, seeks the gift and leaves God to release his gift on the person he chooses, or through a new person he sends to the group. He may reveal who this person is through a word of knowledge. The person with the gift of faith might be at the centre of the praying for the gift. As the gift is released the group are ready to recognize, welcome, and foster the growth of the gift, not least by responding positively when it is used. The details as to how we seek for the gift will vary according to the kind of gift and the group but these basic principles seem to me effective.

I also believe that it is right, from time to time, to ask people what gift they are yearning for and to pray for the Holy Spirit to release that gift. Such a yearning is itself often the preparatory work of the Spirit and the acknowledgement of that yearning an act of obedient faith which enables the gift to be received by the individual. It is also right on occasions that, as leaders, we ask others to pray for new gifts for ourselves.

A third way in which we can foster new gifts is to explain about them and encourage their use generally. In other words prayerfully, supportively and creatively engage a number of people in trying out whether they have a gift. As all are called to witness, and about 10% appear to have the evangelistic gifting, so all are called to serve and some will have a special gift of serving. All are called to encourage and some will have the special gift of encouragement etc. So we can foster the gifts we need by providing a congenial atmosphere in which they can grow. Whether this is discovering gifts or receiving new gifts from the Spirit is practically insignificant. The result is the Church has gifts it didn't have before.

Developing

Gifts need developing by growing understanding and by safe opportunities to use them. Often small groups, or other situations where failure is not too significant, are good contexts in which to develop gifts. It is also good that people with well-developed gifts share themselves with those of similar gifts to guide and encourage development. Some gifts respond to training,[11] others to study and practice, others to prayer. What matters is that gifts are recognized as a trust from God which need responsible nurturing, not only by the person whose gift it has become but also by the leader and, wherever possible, the whole group. Gifts can be stifled as well as developed. Gifts can also be overexposed and people damaged, which normally results in the gift becoming dormant. Hence the development of any spiritual gift is not the responsibility of just the one to whom the gift is given, but also the Christian community in which they live. The leaders have a special responsibility in this area.

Conclusion

The clearer we are about the issue of spiritual gifts the more we realize that we need others and they need us. As our appreciation of spiritual gifts develops we feel our need more powerfully and, hopefully, we can express this feeling to each other. Further, we see the kind of contributions we can each make towards the overall tasks and spot the areas where the group as a whole needs supplementing.

Not only is the significance of the individual person heightened, so also is our awareness of the significance of the interrelationships of people to one another, and the people with tasks. So our next concern is the nature of teams and the effects that teams have on leadership.

Tasks

○×△ 1. Use the Gift Grid to discern your gifts. Use up to four people in checking out your gifts. Prayer partners would be ideal people, so would members of the leadership group you are in.

× 2. Meet with two or three other people from the group and discuss how you can discover and affirm each other's leadership gifts. Try out your approach and evaluate its appropriateness and effectiveness e.g. think of a task or situation, describe ways of leading in it, discuss and express attitudes and feelings. It would be helpful if a summary of this could be sent to me via Bible Society — I want to improve the next edition and I need your help.

○× 3. Design your own cartoon to illustrate the omnicompetent, all gifts blazing, leader you would like to be, in your worst moments! Suggestions to stir the imagination are:

The chief steward — The preacher
The choir leader — The evangelist
The catering convener — The fabric chairman
The leader of the Junior Church

If you are in a group perhaps you could display your cartoons to one another.

○ 4. Consider someone who is your leader. Work out prayerfully and lovingly what leadership gifts you see in them and how these gifts affect the kind of leadership they exercise. During the next week give thanks each day for each gift and ask God to develop their gifts. Ask God to show you what gifts would make their leadership more effective. Do others supply these? If not pray for them to be supplied. Work out how you will know when God answers your prayers.

○ 5. Involve people you lead in doing task 4 for you (this will be a great help for the next chapter).

× 6. As a small group look at a task which needs doing in the church, or by the church in the local community. What kind of gifts (natural and spiritual) and other resources are needed? How can you discover people with the right gifts? How can you develop the gifts when you have discovered them.

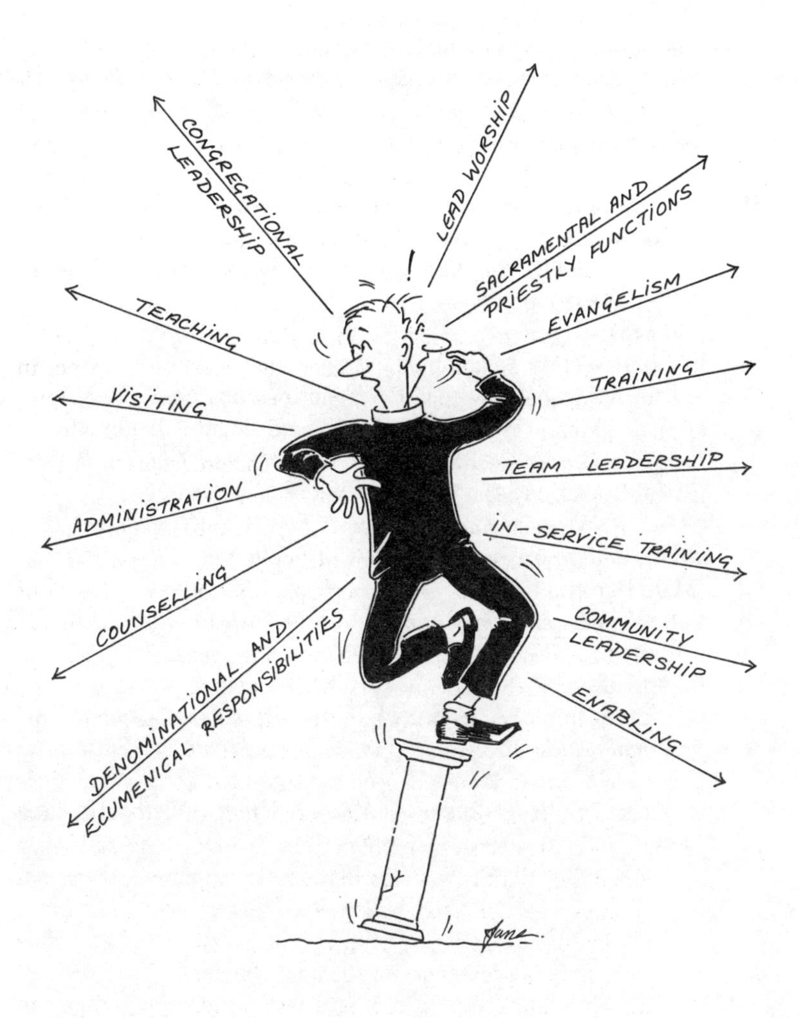
CONGREGATIONAL LEADERSHIP
LEAD WORSHIP
SACRAMENTAL AND PRIESTLY FUNCTIONS
EVANGELISM
TEACHING
TRAINING
VISITING
TEAM LEADERSHIP
ADMINISTRATION
IN-SERVICE TRAINING
COUNSELLING
COMMUNITY LEADERSHIP
DENOMINATIONAL AND ECUMENICAL RESPONSIBILITIES
ENABLING
Jane

References — Chapter 6

1. E Gibbs, *I Believe in Church Growth* (Hodder and Stoughton, 1981), p.356.
2. Cf. Leon Morris, *The Epistle to the Romans* (IVP, 1988), p.438.

> *When we see that God is the giver of all the gifts and that faith is the measure, we will not deny our own gifts either. Being sober-minded means recognizing what God has given us and being zealous in its use as well as humble.*

3. Permission to reproduce it is given. This can be done either by photocopying or by retyping and reproducing.
4. E Gibbs, *Body Building Exercises for the Local Church* (Falcon, 1979), pp.90–94.
5. Ibid p.90.
6. Ibid p.91 section 13 and p.93.
7. For further resources see C P Wagner *Leading Your Church to Growth* (Marc, 1988) pp.132–133 and Joanne Feldmeth *A Leader's Guide — Your Gifts can help the Church Grow* (Regal Books, 1984).
8. Cf. C P Wagner, *Leading your Church to Growth* (Marc, 1984), and *Your Spiritual Gifts Can Help Your Church Grow* (Marc Europe, 1985).
9. C P Wagner, *Leading Your Church to Growth* (Marc, 1984), p.132.
10. Ibid p.132.
11. Cf. for example A Baumohl, *Grow Your Own Leaders. A practical guide to training in the local church* (Scripture Union, 1987).
    R Zuck *The Holy Spirit in Your Teaching* (Victor Books, 1984).

CHAPTER 7

TEAM TALK

"There are fewer areas of living in which we are less successful than that of living and working together. Why?"[1]

Goal

To understand the significance of teams in the purposes of God for today's Church and to prepare to apply this insight.

Aims

1. To appreciate some of the differences between "collections of people" and a team.
2. To see the place that teams have in God's purposes.
3. To understand the value of teams in development and growth within the church.
4. To gain insight about building teams and team leadership.
5. To consider some limitations and dangers with teams.
6. To understand that the transition to a team needs preparation for the leader, the group, and the congregation.
7. To be aware of some of the problems teams will generate for the leaders (and that the leader's problems will generate for the led).

Main Scriptures

1 Corinthians 12; Colossians 1.16–20

Introduction

Few of us like losing. When you are only twelve and the rugby team you play in loses 46–0 it is demoralizing. It is hard on fathers too! As I walked away from the dismal scene I started talking to another father. "Individually they are every bit as good as the opposition, but they don't know how to play together." These words were not the cry of a despondent father, for he was an experienced rugby player and a seasoned referee. He knew that, man for man, they were at least as big and strong, but they lacked instruction, confidence, and co-ordination. The other team played together better, had a clearer grasp of the game and how to play, and had stronger leadership.

A team, although it is composed of individuals, is stronger than its individual elements added together. When chemical elements are joined together as molecular compounds their properties are frequently quite different from the properties of the isolated elements. So it is with people when they become a team.

What is a Team?

How would you define a team? Here is my attempt: "A team is two or more people working cohesively for ends they own".

We can think of the secular world — a netball team, the Cabinet, hospital ward staff, teachers in a school. In various ways they are, or should be, a team. We can think of the church context — the stewards, pastoral visitors, music group, fabric committee. These, too, should be a team.

In some ways teams are puzzling. The netball team is not only the players, it is also the reserves, the coach, the secretary, the manager, and, maybe, even the supporters' club. People can do different things and still be a team. People can be in different places and be part of a team. There would normally be something wrong if all the pastoral visitors turned up at the same house. Equally a number of people together is not necessarily a team. What are the differences between a crowd, a congregation, a group, and a team? It may be easy to list the differences but if a group which should be a team isn't then the results are chaotic. Imagine a ballet company or a church choir which ceases to function as a team! But often groups which should be a team are more like a crowd than a team.

There are many indications in Scripture that God wants his people to be a team. To mention one or two features. Israel is to be organized into a clear tribal structure (Numbers 2). Jesus organized the disciples in various ways to function as a team or teams (e.g. Mark 3.13–18, 6.6–13, 6.39–44). The people of God are to be like a well proportioned and functioning body (1 Corinthians 12).

It is illuminating and fun to take a large sheet of paper and on it draw the outline of a body. Then write on the body the names of the people who correspond to the parts of the body in your church. It's even more fun to do it together as a group. Who are the eyes, ears, nose, mouth, legs, hands, heart etc. in your church or Christian team? How effective is the central nervous system? Does everyone know what everyone else is doing, and do they all know why? (Hint — if, like me, you can't draw why not invite someone to become part of your team of two. You provide the paper and pens and instructions and ask them to draw the outline for you!)

The bigger the issue or aim we have, the more imperative it becomes that we can work as teams. We can move a chair on our own, a wardrobe often needs two people at least, while building a church will take many more! A plan helps a team.

Colossians 1.16–20 is an important statement of God's plan.

> *For through him God created everything in heaven and on earth, the seen and the unseen things, including spiritual powers, lords, rulers, and authorities. God created the whole universe through him and for him. Christ existed before all things, and in union with him all things have their proper place. He is the head of his body, the church; he is the source of the body's life. He is the first-born Son, who was raised from death, in order that he alone might have the first place in all things. For it was by God's own decision that the Son has in himself the full nature of God. Through the Son, then, God decided to bring the whole universe back to himself. God made peace through his Son's sacrificial death on the cross and so brought back to himself all things, both on earth and in heaven.*

It tells us that God has a plan and that it is a very comprehensive one indeed. "God created the whole universe through him and for him… Through the Son, then, God decided to bring the whole universe back to himself." It also implies that God intends to use a team, the body of Christ, which is the Church, to actualize his intention. This makes it imperative that the whole Church and every segment of it becomes as effective a team, and collection of teams, as possible.

Why are Teams from God?

I have already indicated that God appears to value teams and there is a clear pragmatic value in them. But is there more to it? It seems to me there is. Looked at from one perspective God himself is a team — Father, Son and Holy Spirit. Like any good team there is an indissoluble unity, there is effective communication and co-operation, but there is also differentiation of function and even a heightening of individuality. Potentially, teams seem to me to reflect something of the fullness of deity. The family which, on scriptural authority, reflects God's nature, is itself a kind of team, through which we can develop so much more. God creates all of us to be part of his team. We are made in his image, we are incomplete without him. This is even more true for Christians. For instance, "I am the real vine, and my Father is the gardener. …you are the branches…" (John 15.1,5)

Through learning to work in teams we can achieve more, be enriched and experience more of the fellowship which the Holy Spirit brings. Christians should have a higher commitment to teams because the enormity and significance of the task requires them, and we should have a fuller experience of their benefits because the Holy Spirit works for us. However, there are many factors which cause teams to break down and we shall need to deal with these later.

The Value of Teams for Development and Growth

So, accepting the value of teams in general, what are their contributions to growth within the churches and the wider Christian context? For this book on leadership is concerned with growth.

First, a team is potentially stronger than any individual. Members provide support for one another in practical, emotional and spiritual ways. The experience of prayer triplets initiated by Brian Mills is a good illustration of this.[2] By praying together for ends all the members owned there was greater consistency, perseverance, insight and results than people would manage on their own.

Secondly, through teams, skills and experience are readily transferable. On the job training is much in vogue and with good reason. *Evangelism Explosion* is an obvious illustration of this principle. In *Evangelism Explosion* one person trains two others, helps them to learn, supports them through difficulties, takes them out to share the gospel, gradually giving them more responsibility and so on.[3]

Evangelism Explosion illustrates another point. Teams can multiply by dividing. The two trainees can, in their turn, become trainers. Many house groups multiply by dividing. In the context of the house group people discover and develop their gifts until they are, for instance, ready to lead or provide a new venue. Teams make more sustainable growth possible. If one person is ill, or even if the leader dies or is removed some other way, the whole objective of the group is not in jeopardy. Jesus obviously had this in mind in training his disciples.

It is easy to think of scriptual illustrations for these points. But perhaps the most significant point remains to be made. Nobody is perfect but a team can be, or as John Finney puts it

> *Every church is entitled to 10... 10... 10... 10 leadership (in the areas of servant, shepherd, steward and episkopes — elder)... No one person can be a 10... 10... 10... 10 leader ... What you cannot do others need to do.*[4]

In fact, research shows that a balanced team is stronger than the most brilliant individual, or even group of individuals. Dr Belbin has established this and also anaylzed the main functions which need to be carried out in an effective team.[5]

How Teams Work

Following Dr Belbin's work, we can show the main functions required in a good team like this:

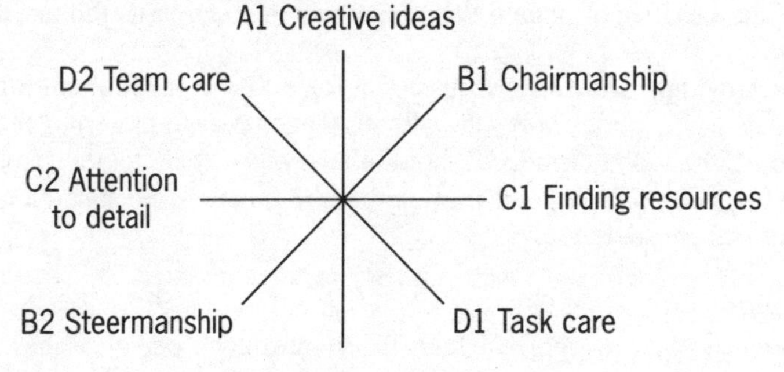

Brief Description:

Functions

A1 Creative ideas — every team needs ideas and suggestions, lots of them. They don't all need to be feasible!
A2 Evaluation of ideas — ideas need to be examined critically for the problems and difficulties
B1 Chairmanship — fair play and decision taking need to happen
B2 Steermanship — sometimes things get stuck, steermanship helps to get them moving even if a bit of manipulation is needed
C1 Finding resources — someone needs to find the people, information and requirements if things are going to happen
C2 Attention to detail — but someone has to keep an eye on the details otherwise confusion and frustration will be major problems
D1 Task care — once decisions have been made they have to become a workable plan and this plan needs modifying throughout the process
D2 Team care — people in the team need to be affirmed especially when the pressure is on. Too much personal hurt causes breakdown of the team

Structure

The diagram indicates opposites. Often people will carry out a preferred function in the team and it relates to their personality and/or spiritual motivational gifting (Romans 12.3–8). They will often be in felt conflict with their opposite; it is because they are doing the opposite task. This structure helps us understand why we find so and so difficult. It is perhaps more helpful to know that this is part of the sacrifice of being in any team which is doing its job properly.

Although Dr Belbin writes about roles I have called them functions. My experience is that, although people have preferred functions, they don't (indeed shouldn't) always stick to their own. What matters for a good team is that the functions are carried out, not that we stick with our role.

Value

We can soon recognize which function(s) each person is best at and, as a team, help one another to do these. However, Dr Belbin's research shows that, for a team to work well, all functions are necessary. Hence, if we are aware of too many people fulfilling some functions and too few others, we can fulfil the servant role by carrying out functions that are not being done. Conversely, if a team is not working well, by looking at which functions are missing, we may see why and be able to rectify the deficiencies.

I find Dr Belbin's insights provide a very helpful diagnostic and corrective guide. However, it is worth noting that different kinds of teams need a different balance. **Doing teams** need more C1 and D1. **People teams** need more D2's, **policy and planning teams** need more A1, A2, B1 and B2's. **Project teams** needs A1 and A2's, C1 and C2. **Long-standing teams** with mixed responsibilities don't need many C1's and B2's until a crisis comes. So it isn't enough to check each function is being carried out. We have to understand the purpose of the team and its requirements. But undoubtedly when we give each team the proper balance of functions it works better. Deny any function and the team runs into trouble.

What Teams Need

Purpose

Dr Belbin's research shows it is helpful for the team members to understand that a team is more than the sum of the individuals. We need to understand we need one another, even if sometimes we don't like one another. We will be more comfortable if we appreciate who is fulfilling which function. But all of this is ineffective unless a team knows and accepts what it is supposed to do. Often frustrations, misunderstandings, and conflicts arise because different members think the group is doing different things. In a Christian context there are often several functions for any given group, so often all the members can be right, but they are also wrong.

Quite often (normally?) the functions of groups within the church are assumed rather than spelt out for all to see and accept. For instance the catering committee. It is obvious to all (isn't it?) that the catering committee is responsible for catering. But are they responsible for providing coffee after the services? Are they supposed to offer it only if requested? Are they in charge of all the catering equipment and the kitchen? Does that mean only they can use it, or can anyone? Do they clean the kitchen, even if the Boys'

Brigade have used it? Who decides their budget? etc. On top of all the practicalities the vicar has probably said, "Ask Freda Smith and Angela Lovelace along, they need the companionship", and has said to Jayne Close, "Get on to the catering committee and bring some spiritual awareness to the group". When people have different agendas there will be a clash of priorities. A clear statement of the responsibilities of the catering committee, their areas of oversight, how their co-ordinator is appointed, how people join etc., together with the acceptance of this by all involved could be helpful.

But the catering committee (and every other team) needs to know how its purpose and aims help the church to fulfil its calling, and how they interrelate to other teams in the pursuit of that calling. They also need to know who has oversight over them. That is, to whom they are accountable and who should support and help them.

Plan

Once a team knows what it is meant to do and why it is doing it, and has accepted this, then it needs to work out how it will accomplish its task. A good plan includes these elements:

1. A workable time schedule
2. Quantification of necessary resources
3. Commitment to ensure all the resources are available at the right time and place
4. Acceptance by individuals of their special responsibility, including a willingness to work with all others necessary to accomplish the task
5. An agreed procedure for dealing with problems
6. A process of checking and reporting progress at appropriate intervals
7. Approval by those in authority for the plan and communication of it to all it affects

A good plan also considers, and seeks to prevent or circumvent, potential difficulties. For instance, if the church mission committee plans to present its programme for evangelism to the church it should foresee the possibility that someone else might use the overhead projector that night, and check it is available. The committee might also realize that the bulb could blow and ensure there is a spare. Obvious, of course, but then many a presentation has been spoilt because... Inevitably, not every disaster can be forestalled. If the storms blow down trees, putting the electricity supply out of action, the overhead projector cannot be used. Unless, of course, someone brings their own generator! However, with the less likely problems there is usually a counterbalance. If the street lights and church lights are out many people probably won't come. Reschedule the presentation and use those who come to pray for evangelism!

People responsible for leading and co-ordinating teams will find two kinds of situation:

1. Setting up a new team to fulfil effectively a role or task
2. Improving the effectiveness of an existing group

These require different approaches.

1. Setting up a New Team

This is, in many ways, the easier. We can give clear definition to the task, the resources, the lines of accountability etc. We can choose the most appropriate people and ensure they have accepted their responsibilities. We can build in a monitoring procedure from the start. However, the members of the team may need help to build relationships and sort out personal tensions. The people selected may not be as suitable for the task as we thought. In committing them to the new task we may well disrupt many other teams which were functioning well, either because we take people from them or because the new team in some way sets up pressure on existing groups.

For instance we decide to set up a music group to accompany the singing and lead the congregation in new worship songs, to teach new songs to the congregation, to enable people with musical gifts to serve God and his people, to broaden the worship experience of the congregation, and especially to provide a more appropriate kind of worship for younger people who have joined the congregation. The music group is accountable to the ministry team with whom they will meet to review progress every month.

It seems straightforward but some from the music group may leave the existing choir. How does the choir react? The new styles of music may not be appreciated by the older members. Some of the present congregation may not wish to encourage these newcomers — their dress is too casual and the special attention they are receiving may be resented. The music group will require space for their instruments and for their presentation. The ministry team need to give time to the meeting — what do they give up? etc.

A clash of personalities can develop between the leader of the instrumentalists and the singers. Songs have to be made available to the congregation and the music licence puts pressure on the budget etc. etc.

The more people there are who understand, and accept, the purpose of the team, realize that adjustments will need to be made, and that the team needs help to grow, the better.

2. Improving the Effectiveness of an Existing Group

This is normally easier to accomplish if the members of the group realize they need help. So, we often need to spend time with individual members helping them to express what they feel about the need for improvements and how these can be made.

There are several, hopefully servant, ways of seeking to help a group, depending to some extent on the causes of the ineffectiveness. Someone can help the group clarify its reasons for existing and find better ways of accomplishing these. There are advantages and disadvantages if the person who does this is not a member of the group. The group can be asked to take on an additional, but associated role, thus giving it a chance to overhaul itself, in all aspects of its life.

New people can be brought in and/or some from the group transferred to other situations. New leaders can make a fresh start and perhaps be given more support and direction from those to whom they are accountable. In this kind of process it is important to affirm the past, that is express valid appreciation for the people in the group and what it accomplishes; to be supportive, not destructive, in the way change is introduced, whether the change is in function or personnel; to help people appreciate the reasons for, and approve, of changes; and surround the whole process with loving prayer.

For instance, if the team running the youth club is not very effective then they could be asked whether they could provide suitable activities for the twelve to fourteen year olds who meet on Sundays but don't have any social activities. This would give the youth club team a chance to consider their range of activities, the resources they need, the possibility of attractive publicity, whether they need to improve their staffing levels, what their aims should be, whether they need a prayer team to provide them with more spiritual momentum. In order to carry out the transition the youth club team would meet with the leaders of the Sunday group etc. Regular meetings could be arranged to monitor progress and support one another, thus improving the integration of the youth club with the church.

In addition to recognizing the differences between starting a new group and improving an existing one, a further distinction helps. Namely, that between a task (or project) and a role. For instance, a task or project has a very specific and usually time limited function; a role is an on-going, people orientated responsibility e.g.

Task To run a six week nurture group for new converts following the mission

Role To run Bible-based home groups once a fortnight

Task To arrange a flower festival for the Sunday in Peace Week next year

Role To arrange flowers for Sunday worship and afterwards distribute them to the sick

Some teams degenerate because they began with a task and never finished. Some teams can be improved by being given a specific task within their role area (e.g. the flower club as above). The skills and input required by the task can become a resource for the role. It can be useful, however, to set up a team for a task to provide a good model for other teams. It can also be a relief (and a model) to end the team once its task is accomplished!

From the foregoing it is clear that teams need good communication both internally (i.e. between the members in the team) and externally (i.e. between the team and those who interact with the team). Few things are more disruptive than poor communication. Few things are more difficult to keep right. It is so easy to forget that whilst I know what is going on inside my head other people won't unless I tell them.

It is also obvious that teams need leading. Having teams makes good leadership more vital. However, the various features of leading can be a shared responsibility. In this case good relations are vital, and care must be taken not to make other members of the team feel excluded or undervalued.

There are two fundamental leadership functions:

1. Ensuring commitment to the task or role
2. Caring for the people in the team

There will often be tensions over these two but failure in either will lead to a lowering of morale and effectiveness.

Difficulties with Teams in a Christian Context

Most Christian groups are, to a large extent, voluntary ones. We have special difficulties to cope with which are potentially damaging and restricting in terms of team efficiency. Here are some of them:

Infrequency

In comparison with a work situation, the frequency of casual and formal meetings is low. The larger the church and the wider its catchment area the more serious this problem becomes. One remedial step is to work even harder to ensure good communication.

Ingathering

Most Christians have a strong commitment to care for one another, which is good. However, we very easily lose our commitment to the team's task or role. The result is we can become inward looking and lose momentum, with the consequence of discontent or apathy. A remedial step is continually to recall the purpose and the vision of the team. A well-designed logo can help, as can an annual review of activities with a commitment to reduce 20% of them.

Infighting

In Christian contexts resources can be scarce, and the more successful we are the more scarce some resources (e.g. space, ministerial time) become. The result can be over-competition for the resources leading to attention seeking, the survival of the most vocal or inter-team warfare (the non-spiritual variety!). Some remedial steps are to build relationships between team leaders, to have a mechanism for the fair allocation of resources and discussion of grievances, and to keep every team aware of and committed to the overall aims of the organization or church.

Good leadership, with the appropriate skills (which may require training to enhance them) and spiritual maturity (which may need opportunities for growth), is therefore vital. People need help to recognize and admit these kinds of problems without being made to feel guilty. Each of them is the converse of a virtue of the Christian Church. Each of them can be overcome.

Smooth Transition

Whether we decide to use teams to prepare for growth, or are forced into using them because of growth, everyone in a church is likely to need help in coping with the transition to a team situation. Over the last few years I have moved from being the leader to being one of a team of five who share the leadership. Even though I was already involved in several teams e.g. the deacons, the Youth Council, the cleaners, the choir, transition has generated some problems for me and the church. For me, these include a felt loss of control, loss of contact with all the congregation and all the organizations, and a decrease in role awareness and identity.

I have discovered that there are often quite unforeseen disadvantages. For instance, I became aware, over a period of a couple of years, that I felt less aware of the well-being of the congregation. This was caused by several factors, some of which were obvious. We had grown numerically, I no longer chaired or attended meetings, we had house groups instead of a mid-week service. But one feature, perhaps the most fundamental, I almost missed. Earlier in my ministry I led and preached at almost every service, twice each Sunday. Whilst doing this I became aware of who was or wasn't there, which then alerted me to find out why. This gave a good feel for the well-being of the congregation, enabling me to pick up danger signals and to take appropriate steps. Now I was one of three main preachers, many others were involved in different aspects of leading worship. I had lost the built-in monitoring device that I used unconsciously. Having located the problem I could share it and involve others in helping to rectify it, but also alert the congregation to the fact that I couldn't have that awareness in the same way. The change created a problem for me and the people. Positively, it also provides others with an opportunity to grow in service.

There are other kinds of problems which moving to a team situation can cause for the leaders. We can feel jealousy. The team may well do it better than the leader. Such jealousy often manifests itself as criticism. There is loss of power, for if we delegate properly we must relinquish power to the team who may go in a different direction, or choose a different way of doing it. Conversely, we may experience greater pressure, for if teams are working well they will generate pressure on leaders to be better organized, more able communicators, more gifted equippers, more open in relationships and, above all, more of an envisioner. If we teach people to do things with a purpose they will want to know what our purpose is.

Just as shared leadership generates problems for those who lead, which the followers need to understand, so shared leadership generates problems for the followers which the leaders need to appreciate. Among them:

Who knows what now
Who decides what now
Who to go to now for whatever
Who is leading now
Is there no one in charge — help!

People, leaders, and led, need to be prepared for the transition to team situations. We need to understand the main repercussions, but also to understand there will be unexpected problems (and bonuses). We need opportunities to face and express our unease to one another. We need to know why changes are being made and that, if and when necessary, they can be modified or even reversed. Most important, we need to help everybody become involved in maximizing the benefits which team thinking and practice can bring, which includes welcoming people when they are expressing their difficulties, even if this feels like criticism.

Tasks/Growth Opportunities

○ 1. What task that you do alone could become a team activity? List at least three for each category. At home e.g. washing up. At work. In the church e.g. preaching/counting the offering/flower arranging. Think through the advantages and disadvantages to you/others in the team/others outside the team, e.g. washing up — involve children in this task. Devise a plan to change from solo to team for one task in each category. (Pick the task which you think would benefit most from each category.)

Advantages			**Disadvantages**		
Self	Others in	Others out	Self	Others in	Others out
Less time? Talk to child and listen	Learn to wash up Feel affirmed Learn to share and accept responsibility	More time to read story to another child	Wait until children ready Stress — breakages	Miss TV programme	Fear that crockery isn't clean Feel excluded from washing up

○ × 2. Get members of a group you are in to write down: what the group exists for; what function each member carries out; to whom the group is accountable, and who supports them.

Then share your insights together and try and reach a consensus. Are there ways in which the group can improve? Is talking about this enough? If not, what action needs to be taken?

○ × 3. Draw structure plans of teams in your church.

i) Three individual teams (who fulfils which role)

ii) Teams of teams (i.e. to show how teams relate/need to relate to one another).

Try and identify strengths and weaknesses in these arrangements. Can you devise ways of helping to improve problem areas? With whom do you need to share these plans and when? What preparation is needed? What will be required to implement them? What resources? What gifts/aptitudes are required by those you involved? What training do they need to be given? Who else needs to be consulted?

If possible do this exercise with at least two other people. Consider allocation of responsibilities, co-ordination etc.

× 4. Games are a helpful way of learning about teams. There are some good ideas helping to build teams at different levels in John Mallison, *Creative Ideas* (Renewal Publications, 1979), p.184. Most industrial and management training schools make use of them. So, meet with two or three others and decide whether to use Mallison's book, help from a training school or equivalent, or devise your own game. Decide what needs doing to fulfil your plan and decide who will do what and when. Try out your chosen game first on yourselves and then on another group. Review its helpfulness.

△ 5. Prayer partners

How much of a team have you become? Consider the openness you have with each other. How can this be improved? Are there problems (felt or otherwise) with communications? How can these be improved? Give your prayer partners a chance to review, renegotiate and reaffirm (or not) their commitment to your and their task.

Pray together!

References — Chapter 7

1. David Cormack, *Team Spirit* (Marc Europe, 1987), p.8.
2. Brian Mills, *Three Times Three Equals Twelve* (Kingsway Publications, 1986).
3. Dr James Kennedy, *Evangelism Explosion* (EE (UK) Ltd, 1977), especially pp.156–160.
4. J Finney, *Understanding Leadership* (Daybreak, 1989), p.69.
5. See A Jay, "Nobody's Perfect", *Observer Magazine,* 20 April 1980, pp.26–28. Your public library may be able to supply a copy of this.

CHAPTER 8

LIMITATIONS TO LEADING

"The rain poured down, the rivers overflowed, and the wind blew hard against that house..." Matthew 7.25.

Goal

To promote realistic awareness of limiting factors for leadership and strategies for maximizing our resources.

Aims

1. To help the central leader to be more aware of the limits and constraints affecting volunteer leaders, and led, in Christian organizations (and vice versa).
2. To help people assess realistically the time they have available for Christian service.
3. To help people choose their priorities and manage their time more effectively.
4. To consider ways of developing commitment, accountability, and mutual support.
5. To introduce the concept of a "succession policy" and its importance in a growth context.

Main Scriptures

Acts 6.1–7; 8.1–4; 11.19–22; 17.5–12

Introduction

We are learning that there are many reasons for getting excited as Christian leaders. There is an answer to the "common round of trivial tasks" which has trapped many central leaders and prevented us from leading our church out of a maintenance only mentality. God does not want us to struggle along. We can begin to resolve the conflicts we feel between leaders and led. We can be released from frustration as we realize God has given gifts to many to use in his Church… and much more.

If I am succeeding in sharing this message we are already moving towards being successful, that is more effective, as leaders which means helping God's people become more effective in kingdom terms, which must mean growth of one kind or another. But there are some potential problems.

Facing Reality

As we dream dreams for the kingdom, which is a good thing to do, we need to come to terms with the limitations of our situation. For instance, Jesus told a story about a farmer who sowed good seed. When it first sprouted he thought he was going to have a bumper harvest, until he realized that half the seedlings were weeds sown by an enemy. Realism caused him to face this hard truth. But it did not lead to despondency. He developed a strategy which still enabled him to reap a good harvest. It was a strategy which recognized the potential problems and overcame them (Matthew 13.24–30). So we need to know what factors limit and restrict us as we seek to develop a wider leadership base in our churches, and how to overcome them.

Jesus is arguably one of the most successful leaders of all times. He managed to get his whole operation off the ground in less than three years. He did not have a church full of professional people on which to draw, nor did he have a government which favoured him. How did he manage to do so much in such a short time? What do you think? Why not jot down a few notes about this now. When you have time read through a gospel and see how many of your ideas fit the picture, and also if you can find any more clues.

As soon as the early Church began to expand it ran into problems. Even though they were empowered and directed by the Spirit they had to be realistic and come to terms with the limitations of their situation. They had internal conflict, restrictions were imposed on their activities, key leaders were removed by the authorities etc. But they did not give up or settle for a defensive strategy. They came to terms realistically with the situation and discovered God had a way out. Read through Acts 6.1–7; 8.1–4; 11.19–22; 17.5–12, and note significant problems and how they were tackled.

Expectations

In many ways one of the hardest limitations to cope with is what people expect. What people expect differs from denomination to denomination and group to group. It is hard because it is like an unseen enemy: restricting, sapping energy, causing conflict, and discontent. It is all the harder because it seems unreal and intangible, but it is very real in its effect. All involved in developing leadership need to be as aware as possible of people's expectations of who can and can't do what. If it is any comfort Jesus found this one hard to cope with too (e.g. Matthew 13.53–58; Mark 8.31–33; Luke 4.23–24, 7.31–50; John 6.14–15).

Being as aware as we can of people's expectations is necessary for effective leadership, but being imprisoned by them is not (see passages above and Acts 6.2). Although they often seem like the unseen enemy sabotaging plans, blowing up lines of good communications, stealing the harvest, and generally hindering the growth we work and pray for they can often be harnessed for growth. Certainly we must avoid slipping from regarding people's expectations as the enemy of growth, to viewing the people who have these expectations as the enemy. All in our community need to be considered potentially as part of the team. It is helpful to discover together what expectations we have and why we hold them. We all need help to see other ways of doing things, other ways of leading, and people will need time to come to terms with these things. Our expectations may seem very threatening to others, so they deserve Christian respect, support, and consideration. I was greatly helped by a discussion I had with a person in a senior management position in the health service. He drew the following plan.

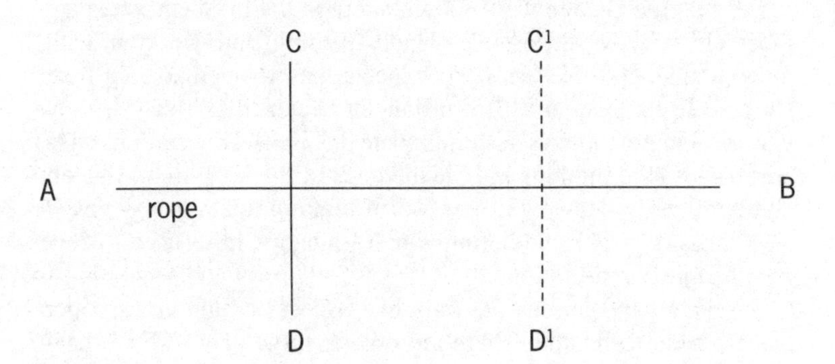

He explained that if B wants to move the line C–D to C^1–D^1 the obvious, natural way is to pull the rope and pull A with him. The problem is that when A feels the pull against him he will pull in the opposite direction: so resistance grows. The harder B pulls the harder A pulls — but in the opposite direction. (Even relatively straightforward things like changing the times of services, or the hymn books we use, can generate enormous resistance; even a different typewriter in the office!) B may do well to stop pulling when he encounters A's resistance and not pull harder. Bs, if they are leaders, may well feel that to stop pulling is to resign leadership and to surrender to A and his expectations. But if B stops pulling, explains to A why he wants to move C–D to C^1–D^1, and especially if B can affirm A and involve him in the process, then A may well help B, or at least not resist. It might even be that A will convince B that C–D should be left as it is. If this is so it is better not to move it, and waste all the energy! In other words it is better to avoid adding force to force. Rather, seek to diminish resistance through understanding, affirmation, and co-operation.

Little is lost in this process apart from time (which occasionally is crucial) and a sense of great victory (or even valiant defeat) by leaders who have expended unnecessary energy, and in reality drained the resources of the kingdom and been lured into ineffectiveness. We need to remember that normally the leaders are suggesting and generating changes. It will feel to others that the leaders have power and are dominating them, giving them a sense of powerlessness which can be very threatening. It is salutary to recall situations where change was imposed on us. To consider how and why we responded as we did. Even when changes are necessary and become accepted, or even welcomed, by those who initially resisted, it is not sufficient for us as Christian leaders to be able to say or think "We were right", we need to know for ourselves that the change was brought about in the most Christian and most effective way possible. Understanding and working with, rather than opposing, people's expectations is a great help here. Even so Jesus' responses, for instance to Peter in Mark 8.33, show that we cannot always accommodate people's expectations. The purpose of the kingdom and the methods of the king are ultimately non-negotiable. However, it is worth looking again at the gospel references on p.117 and noting which strategies Jesus used to cope with people's expectations.

People's expectations are only one aspect of limitations which leaders need to handle. There are others, some of which we have already considered. For instance, as leaders our personal gifts and skills are limited — this is God's plan for his church! It ensures, or at least provides, the opportunity for other people and their gifts to be valued, developed, and used. Our particular leadership style, or indeed our personality, may be a problem, or the leader's response to others may be a problem for the leader and the whole group. We have given hints about handling these sets of limiting factors in "Team talk".

We already have considerable resources for overcoming the restrictions on our capacity to lead, or be part of, an effective team. But there are a few more crucial aspects, so we now give consideration to these.

Time Enough

How much time do full-time Christian workers have whether they are vicars, Youth for Christ workers, Bible Society Regional Support Representatives etc.? The obvious answer is they have twenty four hours a day and fifty two weeks a year. At least this is what it can seem are people's expectations — especially this is what it can seem like to their families! They "should" be available whenever they are needed by the organization. Some of us try to live with that expectation. But we don't have to and we shouldn't. But we do have a responsibility to help other people understand their expectations and, if possible, help them to cope with the fact that leaders are not always available.

The telephone means that leaders can be contacted from the comfort of their own home (at the discomfort of their own home). What is the answer? For some an answer-phone, for some an office or office hours, for some a clear indication as to when they are and are not available, for some a deputy or associate who covers for them. Again, if a team of people help the full-time leader and those he leads come to terms with the issue of time availability it is likely to be more effective for all concerned, and will lessen the felt guilt of the leader who probably, like me, finds it harder to say "No" to requests or demands from outside than to his family!

But if it is easy for others to assume that full-time Christian leaders are available whenever anyone wants them, it is just as easy for leaders to think that Christians in secular employment are available whenever they want them, other than the thirty seven and a half hours they are at work, or if they are housewives any time after breakfast! For the real good of the kingdom we all need to be realistic about the time (when, as well as how much) that we can rightly give or ask for. An underlying issue here is accepting that people are committed to Christ as fully as they can be. Often we use the time issue as a test of this, or a means to it. Probably this is not as helpful as it first seems. It is better to tackle the time issue for its own sake, and help people examine and develop their commitment in a different context. If we do see commitment as a hindrance to the offer or use of time for Christian work then we should be gentle but open about this and not keep it as part of a hidden agenda.

Once we recognize that time is not limitless for anyone, full-time or not, then being realistic about the time any task will take is important. In my experience almost every task takes longer than we at first think. So it is important that this can be reviewed and appropriate responses worked out.

Among possible responses to such a situation are:

1. Requesting/offering more time (however, we all need to be realistic. This means less time for something else. What will it be and is it right this should go? Who else should be involved in assessing and deciding it is right?)
2. Re-allocate responsibilities. This can be done by redefining the task, giving a longer period of time for the task to be accomplished, or by introducing some time efficiency feature (e.g. "Don't write up minutes of the meeting, phone me").
3. It can also be done by involving more people, or different people. However, organizing and supporting people also takes time and energy and this shouldn't be ignored.
4. Becoming more efficient. I like David Cormack's suggestions.[1] He has two key words, one for handling paper — AIRS, the other for coping with people — GRACES. I cannot better his explanations.

A— Action. Reply now or file and sort on a daily basis.
I — Information. Read at a time suitable for you but do not use prime time.
R — Reading. Long letters and circulars, use spare moments when travelling etc.
S — Scrap. Junk mail, don't bother opening.

G — Greet only. Say, "Hi," and go back to your work.
R — Receive. Say, "Come in. Nice to see you," and then go

on with your work.

A — Accompany. Say, "Hello, glad you stopped by, so-and-so was looking for you. Let me take you along," then get on with your work.

C — Confer. Recognise that this is someone who needs your time as a priority and give him ten minutes.

E — Embrace. Put on the kettle, for this one is serious and urgent.

S — See off. Make it quite clear that you are busy and cannot stop your work, but would be delighted to spend time later.

Although we cannot create more time in a day we can often use our time more effectively. Careful planning can be advantageous here. One of our members is a fitted kitchen specialist. He knows that the first thing that has to be fitted is the floor covering, everything else goes on top of that. He also knows what the lead time for getting that floor covering is. He has to work very hard (and gently) to get his customers to choose the floor covering early enough. It is usually the last thing they want to decide. If he fails the whole process is delayed. Of course he has contingency plans so that he does not waste his time completely. But he knows careful planning saves everyone his time, and that also means money. However, he had to balance efficiency with courtesy. If he offends his customers by being too pushy they can go elsewhere!

We also have to be comprehensive in calculating the time cost of activities. It may seem that we shall save time using a car instead of catching the bus. The journey may take ten minutes instead of thirty. However, we shouldn't neglect the time it takes to get the car out of the garage, the time to park the car (and the anxiety of finding a space, or avoiding the traffic wardens!), the need to clean and service the car etc. There are often less obvious factors which we need to dig out to be realistic. Often it is better to try an alternative for a few weeks and then assess on the basis of experience. (So don't sell the car too soon!)

In seeking to save time it is also good to ask others to monitor the consequences. This is particularly true as far as "wasted" time is concerned. We can gain an hour by getting up earlier but we may become more irritable, our health might suffer, our partner might resent the fact we are not there when they wake up, we may go to bed earlier to compensate and the family miss out on our company. Involving others in this evaluation helps us in realism, it also helps them in understanding and acceptance, thus lessening the risk of time wasting conflicts! It is important that we consider others in our evaluations. If we leave a meeting promptly as it finishes we save time talking but others may feel we are unsociable and unfriendly. In taking them into account we may decide that it wasn't time wasting but a valuable time of discovery and affirmation. Here we save time in a different way when we realize the value of what we are doing!

It is helpful to have an objective record of how we use our time. Keeping a diary with a note of what we are doing at fifteen minute intervals is a good start. Probably we need to keep it for a seven day period. (It is also useful, on the basis of this diary, to quantify the time spent in various activities — sleeping, eating, maintaining relationships, reading, working, playing with children etc.) Once we have quantified the time spent then we can ask ourselves such questions as: "Is this really how I want to spend my life?", "Is this really the way God wants me to use my week?", "How does God want me to change?", "Can I accomplish more if I re-allocate my time?" Such an exercise can be quite revealing. It may help us see more clearly where we can recover time to use for God's work. It also provides us with a record to check for progress in a few months' time. It does require a great deal of honesty and commitment.

Our prayer partners can be great allies in helping us make changes in habits. Most of us will need them to check on us to ensure we do not slip back into old ways. It can be very hard work to gain time but it is worth the effort. It brings personal fulfilment, often more Christlikeness of character and effectiveness for the kingdom.

Priorities

However efficient we become in using time we will also have to choose our priorities. Indeed, it is part of the process of effective use of time. As Christians we shall always be seeking to answer the question "What does God want me to do?" rather than "What would I like to do?", although the words of the covenant service help to remind us that there will not always be a conflict here.[2] The more we are controlled by God's Spirit the less this conflict will be experienced, although we should never expect to be conflict free (see Mark 14.32–42).

In trying to evaluate priorities we must, of course, be open to God's special directions which may come directly (in which case it is good to check them out with trusted, prayerful friends), or through the suggestion or invitation of Christian leaders.

In practice I find there are some fundamental factors to consider in establishing God's priorities for my life:

1. The need. Is the task to be accomplished vital for the kingdom?
2. My gifts. Do they equip me for my part in this task?
3. Others. Are other people available who could do this as well as/better than I, whose commitments allow them to do so more easily?
4. Do other people see me as their first choice for this job, and what kind of motives and influences bring them to this decision?
5. What are my preferences in all this? My preferences will reflect the kind of person I am, and the calling I have from God.
6. If I take this on who can replace me in my present position? (Often we need to act in faith over this one).

Clearly, in assessing our priorities we need to take careful account of other people to whom we are accountable. If we are leaders we may need to help others assess their priorities and we need to know to whom they are accountable, always remembering that those include family, employers, and friends as well as the Christian community. It is important when assessing priorities to include others in the process as early, as fully, and as openly as possible. Once we have decided not only what needs doing, and in what order, but also what we should do, we are ready to delegate to other people.

Delegation

As we grow in our leadership, and as the opportunities for which we are responsible develop, it becomes increasingly necessary for us to learn how and what to delegate. Delegation is a vital art for any leader to practise. We should therefore be encouraging others to do so.

There are some fears which hold many of us back from delegating. We need to look at these and, if they influence us, need to receive God's help to handle them. Many of them are related to people's expectations of us and/or our inability to trust others. Think for a few minutes about the issues which come to mind with a simple delegation. For instance, asking a seven year old child to go to the local shop to fetch a newspaper, a box of matches, and three first class stamps. Here are a few:

1. What will the neighbours think? That I am lazy and irresponsible?
2. How would I cope if they were injured en route? Could I forgive myself?
3. Is it legal for a seven year old to buy matches?
4. Will they remember which newspaper I want, spend, or lose the change, or be duped by the shopkeeper?
5. Will they get back in time with the stamps for me to post Grandma's birthday card?
6. What if they are tempted to light a fire with the matches?

Isn't it amazing that God has entrusted us with the message of reconciliation! He believes that delegation is worthwhile. It certainly is, but it is not opting out or an easy option. Often, particularly in the early stages, it is harder work than doing it ourselves. But delegation develops other people and extends our effectiveness.

Good delegation is assisted by certain factors. Here there are: a clear description of the task, the resources available, the time and energy required, and to whom those delegated report and when. ("Please bring me a Guardian newspaper, a large box of matches, like the one in the kitchen, and three first class stamps. I've jotted them down on this piece of paper. The money is on the table by the door. Go to Jones' so you don't have to cross a road. Can you please come straight back as I need the stamps for Granny's birthday card. When you give me the change I will give you your pocket money" etc.)

Good delegation requires free acceptance of the task and its responsibilities. ("Are you happy to do that for me? I'm so glad I can trust you and we can tell Granny you went for the stamps.")

Good delegation is helped by frequent reviews which should be seen not as a session of criticism but an opportunity to support and review those to whom tasks are delegated. Preferably such review opportunities should be fixed in advance so they are seen as positive times and not a crisis management technique, although people should feel free to come to us when they need support. ("Before you go, can you let me know you've found the money.")

Good delegation is helped by providing "opt out clauses". That is, opportunities for people to relinquish their responsibilities without feeling they have failed. This leaves people free to continue to work with us on other tasks. If we ask people to do more than they can cope with that is our misjudgment not their fault!

Good delegation is helped by arranging and encouraging support of all kinds, including prayer and approval. ("Can you manage on your own or do you want John to go with you?")

Good delegation is never opting out. Others should receive the rewards, we should take the responsibility, especially when things go wrong. ("Don't worry that the change fell down the drain, I should have given you a purse to put it in. Granny will be pleased you got the stamp...")

Good delegation is vital for the kingdom and the more we see the kingdom God's way the more important it becomes (Matthew 9.35–10.42). As this passage shows, good delegation is helped by honesty about possible difficulties!

A Succession Policy

As we delegate tasks and responsibilities properly we are developing other people's abilities. Such development is necessary, not only because of growth in the size of the task, but also because leaders are constantly on the move. For instance, not only moving area because of jobs but also because of changing needs and responsibilities, changing interests, changing stages of life, and ultimately death. Even in a non-growth situation we need to provide more and more leaders. When we are planning for growth this is even more the case.

A succession policy is an agreed understanding about the need for, and provision of, leaders and the process through which they come into leadership. There are many possible succession policies and I have seen most of them at work in the Church. Among them are:

1. Jackdaw. Steal other people's leaders or those they have trained.
2. Ostrich. Bury our heads in the sand and hope new leaders will emerge from somewhere.
3. Robin. Chase other possible leaders off our territory to preserve our status.
4. Cuckoo. Plant your potential leaders for others to nurture, then grab them back.

These are probably not the best kinds for Christians.

It is better if there is some overall strategy in our organization about developing leaders, otherwise demands can all go in the direction of the few obviously able people, and others who, with encouragement and training, have something to offer, get overlooked. So some forum where consideration to these matters can be prayerfully given is important. It is also important that resources of time, energy, and money are budgeted for training and equipping people. One valuable and economic way of training people is to ask each leader to work with two other deputies with whom they will share insights, experience, and spiritual growth, as well as provide opportunities for the two to ask questions and contribute by doing. This is often known as the apprenticeship model.

If it is agreed that some kind of planning for developing leaders is desirable then the issues which need to be thought through will include, what needs for leadership can we foresee, and how can we discover this accurately without frightening the present leaders? Who selects suitable people; how can we avoid only asking the obviously talented and overlooking others; how can we know what aptitudes people have; how can we avoid inter-group conflict over good leadership potential; what expectations do we give to these trainees? What training is needed and how best can they receive it? Do we send them on courses; do we train "in house"; do we give them books and let them get on with it; or do we use the apprenticeship model? How are people called, appointed, and recognized? Which is the appropriate group and method? How do we build in proper accountability? What checks and safeguards are required? How do we maintain continuity and quality among the leadership?

A useful book to prompt further thought and provide more specific guidance is Anton Baumohl, *Grow Your Own Leaders* (Scripture Union, 1987).

Conclusion

I think it is a good aim for leaders to seek to work themselves out of a job by delegating and equipping others for all their responsibilities. From my experience this is one aim which we will never fulfil but which we must always seek to fulfil.

Tasks

○ × 1. Read through a gospel and note key factors as to why Jesus was a successful leader. How important were the use of time, sticking to priorities, succession policy etc? How can these features influence your leadership?

○ 2. Write a letter inviting a person to become a member of a team doing something you are responsible for. Then:

— Assess this letter from the viewpoint of the recipient (e.g. does it tell you all you need to know, how does it make you feel, who do you need to consult, what changes will you need to make, how can you assess this request in terms of your priorities?)

— As the originator of the letter work out what qualities the person will need, what safeguards are there both for the person and for the task?

× 3. Make use of the following group Bible study exercise. Please adapt the directions as you wish e.g. if you don't meet as a group ask people to write down their observations and give them to you. However, try to adapt in line with the aims i.e. to gather biblical insights on the issues in this chapter and to practice the skills mentioned.

Split a large group into smaller groups and hand out one set of instructions to each group. Explain that you will share your insights in ten minutes (would it help to have a coffee break?).

i) You have 10 minutes for this task
What can we learn Luke 10:1–12 about delegating tasks to others?
Please appoint someone a) to give a 2 minute presentation of your findings and b) to suggest another suitable biblical passage.

ii) You have 10 minutes for this task
What can we learn from Mark 6.33–34 about delegating tasks to others?
Please appoint someone a) to give a 2 minute presentation of your findings and b) to suggest another suitable biblical passage.

iii) You have 10 minutes for this task
What can we learn from Mark 3.1–6 about the effect of people's expectations?
Please appoint someone a) to give a 2 minute presen-

tation of your findings and b) to suggest another suitable biblical passage.

iv) You have 10 minutes for this task
What can we learn from 2 Timothy 2.1–7 about training others?
Please appoint someone a) to give a 2 minute presentation of your findings and b) to suggest another suitable biblical passage.

v) You have 10 minutes for this task
What can we learn from Acts 13.4–5, 13–14; 15.36–41; 2 Timothy 2.11 about developing commitment and mutual support?
Please appoint someone a) to give a 2 minute presentation of your findings and b) to suggest another suitable biblical passage.

vi) You have 10 minutes for this task
What can we learn from John 13.1–5, 12–17 about developing commitment and mutual support?
Please appoint someone a) to give a 2 minute presentation of your findings and b) to suggest another suitable biblical passage.

vii) You have 10 minutes for this task
What can we learn from Acts 6.1–7 about the use of time?
Please appoint someone a) to give a 2 minute presentation of your findings and b) to suggest another suitable biblical passage.

○ 4. Decide to keep an "efficiency diary" as described on p.122. When will you do this? When will you prepare your seven day planner? Who will you share this plan with?

△ ✕ 5. Fill out the list (Table 6) of reasons for not delegating. Then consider ways of getting others to help you with your difficulties, either by sharing it with your prayer partners, or in your group.

References — Chapter 8

1. David Cormack, *Seconds Away* (Marc Europe, 1986), pp.90–93.
2. See *A Covenant Service,* The Baptist Union. "In some we may please Christ and please ourselves, in others we cannot please Christ except by denying ourselves."
3. David Cormack, op.cit. p.96.

Table 6

I Do Not Delegate Because	**Applies to me**	
	Yes	No
1. No-one can do it as well as I can.		
2. I cannot trust anyone.		
3. No-one has the skills.		
4. It's my responsibility.		
5. It takes too long to explain.		
6. It is quicker doing it myself.		
7. I have been let down too often.		
8. I like doing it.		
9. People expect me to do everything.		
10. I have more flexibility if I do things myself.		
11. I work better on my own.		
12. No-one has any spare time.		
13. No-one will accept the work.		
14. I prefer to make the decisions.		
15. I like to keep control.		
16. I have no time to keep chasing people.		
17. It is more bother than it's worth.		
18. I cannot afford a mistake.		
19. *		
20. *		
TOTAL		

* I am delegating these two to you. Write your own excuses![3]

CHAPTER 9

"POP GOES THE LEADER"

"Are you a limiting factor in your church?"[1]

Goal

To enable leaders to grow into a more adequate kind of leadership as their group develops.

Aims

1. To alert all involved, especially the central leader, to the fact that their role can change.
2. To understand something of other leadership roles that become more necessary with overall growth, and development of a more adequate leadership base.
3. To provide reference to further materials as a resource to extend the scope of 2.
4. To help the central leaders prepare themselves and others in their group for the impact of these changes both emotionally and organizationally.

Main Scriptures

Acts 20.17–38

Introduction

So now the vicar no longer writes, edits, types, prints, collates, and distributes the church magazines, what *does* he do? But he no longer preaches all the sermons, says the prayers or distributes the bread and wine at communion either, so what *does* he do? But he had a pastoral care team etc. etc. So what *does* he do?

In my church the answer you might get from people is "He

thinks up new jobs for us to do!" As long as people can see how the jobs contribute to the calling of the people of God, and are carried out by people who want to fulfil that calling, and are equipped for those tasks, progress can be made. We are not, however, making work for work's sake, to reduce the church's non-employed statistics! Real jobs for real people is what we are after, and people who are fulfilled because they are aware their job is making a significant contribution to a whole, whose value is eternal.

But if we return to our vicar. What would his job be? As far as the magazine is concerned he might well be supporting the editors by making sure they had the right resources and by letting them know of people with a gift for writing. He would ensure they review their methods of production and that they choose the most appropriate ones. He would help those who collated the magazine understand the importance of what they were doing, and those who distributed the magazine to develop the pastoral opportunity of their situation.

But, even more significantly, he would be helping the church answer questions like, what is our magazine trying to do? Is this the best purpose for it? What else could we do with it? Do we need a supplementary form of communication? Is our purpose a good purpose? Do people understand its purpose? Is there a better one? What factors would make it better? Do we accomplish our purpose? If so, to what extent? How can we use Christian literature more effectively? What does our distribution method achieve? Are there people who need access to the magazine who don't get it? Could a different approach to the distribution make a worthwhile contribution to the aims of the church? How do we recruit and train those who take it out? Can we use this, or other means of creating or using Christian materials, to make it easier for people to understand the gospel and respond to it? What effect should changes in the life of the church have on our magazine? How can we monitor these and plan for change?

Of course, all the time the vicar will be looking for people who can take over these concerns for him. The whole process of talking the issues through will be preparing the ground for this. Through such conversations it will become clear who has special sensitivity, awareness, and aptitude, and in which areas. It might be a useful step to set up a small group to look at, say, the church's communication needs, internal, and external.

This would require a brief and terms of reference. It would raise issues far beyond the boundaries of the newsletter and so might slow up short-term changes to the newsletter. It might, therefore, be better to have a group who look at the purpose, production, and distribution of the newsletter. Even though the vicar might be the person who is initiating the in-depth thinking about an issue, he is not always the best person to be seen doing the initiating. It might be much easier and more effective if the newsletter editor is encouraged to do the initiating.

So, whilst the vicar may no longer write all the magazine, or in fact any of it, he will be helping to ensure that the magazine is accomplishing its God given task and that all involved — writers, editors, producers, and readers — understand and welcome this. He will be concerned that the magazine is making its proper contribution to the life of the church.

What is true for a specific and limited area of the church's life, like the newsletter, is true for any other. The more complex these areas are, and the more central to the church's calling, the more crucial the central leader's role becomes. But why should the vicar pay so much attention to the newsletter? It may be that he has a systematic plan to review the various aspects of the church's life, and it is now the turn of the newsletter or communications. If not, perhaps the vicar or the central leader should encourage the church's leaders to draw up such a plan. This would be a similar procedure to that of ensuring that a car is regularly serviced for maximum efficiency and reliability. Or, like a house, for which people have a five year plan for redecoration and upgrading, taking rooms in turn, but also including the outside decorating and redesigning of the garden. So the church needs an agreed plan to review every aspect of its life.

However, it might be that the newsletter is under the search light because comments from a number of people focus attention on the issue, or key people relinquish their responsibilities for the newsletter, or even that people come along and offer to help in some way. This would be similar to something going wrong with the car requiring emergency treatment, or damage by high winds, or a burst pipe needing immediate action in the home.

Of course, in focusing attention on the newsletter the central leader has to be aware that other areas of the church's life will not be receiving the same in-depth attention. So, our vicar will need to be evaluating priorities, and neither allow himself to be trapped by the five year plan (i.e. be unable to respond to the needs of the developing situation, so flexibility is required), nor to be pressurized into doing something just because a few people pass comments (i.e. become a monitor of change rather than a manager, so maturity is required).

Hopefully, whilst reading through this we shall have been thinking "Is this really the vicar's job?" and "This requires a team of people to handle it effectively", or "Who can I involve to work with me on this so that they can look at the next issue, or so I can delegate this task in five years' time?" Which brings us to our next subject.

Creating Space

As the illustration of the newsletter shows, the central leaders always need to be creating space for themselves so that they can be moving into higher levels of leadership, but always with a view to serving the community of God's people with whom they work and enabling others to use their abilities etc. The central leader (some far more than others!) will need help from many people to achieve this, not least from those who lead with them. Many Christian leaders know how difficult it can be to find daily space with God. Without this opportunity vision and motivation for all will suffer.

But other kinds of space are also equally necessary. Often some plan for study or reflection will be helpful. For instance a week every three months released from all normal responsibilities, or three months leave for study every seven years. Obviously this needs to be agreed with the organization they lead, its purpose understood and some way of feeding the benefits back to the organization should be found so that the church or organization experiences the benefits.

I find the phrase used by a minister involved with the Coventry Industrial Mission very telling. He speaks of "loitering with intent": by which he means being free to see, and respond to, significant opportunities for God's kingdom. For this ever to be a possibility we shall need to work very hard at an effective succession policy and become very good at sorting out our priorities, otherwise we shall quickly lose any space we gain. But the space the central leader needs is not only to do with time and energy, it is also acceptance by the community he or she is called to lead. This issue is vital. If this is not accomplished any change in the leader's role will create much friction and can easily be counter-productive.

It is often helpful to start with a fairly concrete task like the newsletter and help the church see that other people may have more appropriate skills. Then, as the finished project improves, as they find the vicar has another kind of contribution to make, etc. a model has been provided for other developments in leadership. It is also important to find the right issue to use! If the newsletter is sacrosanct, or if the newsletter editor is very dogmatic and dominant, then normally it is better to use a less controversial issue — one that is more likely to result in positive and successful change. Eventually after time, with progress and prayer, we will be ready to handle the obstinate issues.

How can we know where to begin? There will be many factors. Amongst them, what is appropriate for the church's life? i.e. What needs attention now and what is likely to have a "knock on" effect? To what is God drawing attention, what seems ripe for change? Clearly a decision is more likely to be arrived at after prayer and, where possible, discussion with other leaders. It is important to be as aware as possible of the things that will hinder change, (cf. p.118 on reducing resistance), but we must not become like the rabbit in the headlights of the car, paralysed by these factors. Some hindrances to change are specific to that local congregation, often depending on the previous central leader's role. Clearly people's expectations are a major factor here. If the previous central leader has been around for many years (and even more so if they continue to be around after relinquishing their post), and if they were either successful or popular, they will have generated very strong expectations in the congregation. It is worth remembering our discussion about handling resistance on pp.117–118. But there are some additional points to work with. Always honour the previous person, never criticize or concur with criticism. Seek to develop, not destroy, their plans wherever possible and ensure that all concerned understand this is the intention. Build on their successes and give them a share in the credit for your developments — they will have made them possible. It is much better for the central leader, and far more appropriate in the Christian context, to perceive the predecessor as an ally and not a threat.

Whilst some hindrances to change are mainly related to factors in the local situation, others are apparently much more determined by the denomination. This is particularly true for those tasks which are labelled "ordained". Obviously it is important not to be in conflict with the proper church authority, but there is still much more room for manoeuvre than I would have thought possible. For instance, one Roman Catholic priest makes extensive use of members of his congregation, not only in preparation of parents for the christening service, but also within the service. In Anglican communion services lay people are involved more and more, not only in distributing the elements, but in leading parts of the service, or in taking communion in people's homes. Anglican lay people function as chaplains in city centre shops. At one time the Baptist minister would always chair the deacons' meeting but there is room for change here too.[2]

Careful preparation of those receiving the change, as well as those involved in leading, is vital. The more people there are involved, the more vital the planning, communication, and organization become. But other kinds of leadership become vital too. It is to consideration of some of these central leaders' roles we now turn. Remember these are not just time fillers, they are vital for a church to be healthy and growing, which is what God calls us to be.

Higher roles

Envisioner — Keeper of the Visions

"Leadership without vision is doomed to mediocrity and even failure."[3]

Every organization, and particularly the Church, needs a vision of what it is meant to be, where it is meant to go, and what it is meant to accomplish on the way. I say "particularly the Church" for several reasons. First, it has a very high calling and if it fails it is a serious matter for God and the whole world. Secondly, because of its inherent commitment to care for people it can easily lose direction and seek to avoid the tensions which a vision creates. Thirdly, its vision is so large at one level that it is not always easy for the church to own its vision concretely enough for the vision to provide the momentum it should. Some leaders will express the vision and people will opt in. Others will consult and clarify the vision people have. But Christian organizations need people who will help them to see and be committed to their God-given vision. Inherent in this task is that of providing motivation for God's people to keep on doing God's work. A proper succession policy will lead to a desire to develop the prophetic ministry within the church, to enable fresh vision to be received, and for the organization to be evaluated *vis-à-vis* its vision.[4]

Teacher

The central leader will normally have a theological education. One of the main roles will be to pass on this in-depth understanding of the faith to others. What God is and what God wants needs to be based on objective teaching. But the teacher also needs to pass on the value of having such an understanding — that is, how a grasp of the faith operates in, and for, the life of the people of God.

A succession policy here will mean a commitment to "train others also" (e.g. 1 Timothy 4.11–16; 2 Timothy 2.2), to ensure that the church's education and training policy is soundly based and that people have access to resources (books, tapes, videos, a variety of learning contexts, the benefit of other people's teaching gifts etc.) to enable them to become fluent in the content and inner logic of their faith.

Director

"Directing is the stuff that converts goals into action and dreams into reality"[5]

Every Christian organization has a vital job to do for the kingdom of God; if not, it has no right to exist. Therefore we cannot be content with some theory, however grand and glorious. There is a real need to help the church, at every level, turn its dreams and theory into practice. Discussion must progress to decision, and decisions to deeds that make a difference. The central leader has the task of overseeing the many facets of planning and organization. Even more crucially, the central leader should ensure that these are, and remain, the servants of the God-given vision and the God-given people. Efficiency, organization, and procedural rules can so easily become the masters and they need to remain the servants. Succession policy here will lead to a desire to involve others in these responsibilities and to train deputies who are acceptable to the church or group.

Facilitator

Jim Eliot says "Remember always that God has taught you the importance of a *building* ministry."[6]

There are two main features to this role. First, that of encouraging people to recognize, receive, and utilize their gifts in harmony with others. Secondly, that of equipping and developing others, or at least seeing that this is happening. It also involves recognizing what a situation requires. Just as a fire needs a match before it will burn, so often a group needs a particular spark before it will function properly. Equally the match needs the fire. So often a group needs someone to really get it going and that someone will flourish in that group. In other words the facilitator has the task of maximizing people's potential for the service of the kingdom. This task is broader than it might at first appear and requires both sensitivity and strength. This is because the kingdom is always bigger than our organizations so we may well need to encourage people to move on. This will mean varied things, from giving less time to the church and more to their family, to leaving our organization to develop in, or serve in, some other capacity.

Succession policy here will mean welcoming others into pastoral situations where talents can be discovered and then made available. It will mean using others to pass on their skills and expertise. It will mean being willing to encourage people from outside our group to come in to equip it.

Modeller

"Whether we like it or not, we are being watched. And... followed."[7]

Our leader is the incarnate Son of God. Ultimately what we are is of greater significance than what we say or do. Hence the vital importance of Chapter 3. But what we are includes what we say and do, as well as how and why we do it. John Wimber, in one of his tapes, tells how he came to see that his church had become an enlarged version of himself and he didn't like what he saw. Modelling had taken place (in his case, on a large scale) as it almost inevitably will do. But since then he has gone on to model his ministry in a very beneficial way. Every leader, at whatever level they operate, needs to be aware of the influence, for better or worse, we have on other people. The Christian person we are becoming is a vital contribution to the leadership of the Church and, like John Wimber, we need to be ready for God to change us so that others can learn from us in a constructive way.

Succession policy here will mean welcoming people into a close relationship with us, where they can experience our life and where they are encouraged to minister to us to improve our Christian life, so that the model is always becoming more Christlike. Succession policy will mean an emphasis on the quality of the Christian person throughout the Church (Mark 3.13–15; 1 Thessalonians 2.1–12).[8]

Evaluator

As Christians we want to avoid being harshly judgmental and critical about people, and negative about situations. However, we can afford to be honest, because the outcome is in God's hands. We also need to be honest. We can be so concerned to be kind that we seek to avoid, at any cost, the pain which is necessary for growth. Jesus was often very honest with his disciples and others, warning them of dangers, reprimanding them for their lack of faith, or bringing weakness out into the open (Matthew 10.16–25; 24.4–8, Mark 4.35–40; 9.19, Luke 6.22–26; 9.46–48).

Christians also tend to exaggerate (how many people really were at the meeting, how many people really became Christian disciples at the evangelistic event, how much did we learn at the Bible study!?). If we are to be effective we need a Christlike realism. We are free to fail. We can profit from mistakes — but only if we know we are making them. Therefore someone needs to be evaluating what is happening in order to correct mistakes and avoid dangers. Someone, indeed, needs to create the ethos where evaluation is welcomed! The evaluator needs to ensure that all aspects of the work are monitored. This requires a commitment to measure and, in the light of the results, to modify plans accordingly. The measuring of results will be more illuminating if the aims are also quantified. A succession policy here may well begin by getting others to evaluate us (see Task 5). In using David Cormack's *Seconds Away*,[9] I involved someone else in my fight for greater efficiency. This led them to want to work through the book also. Being willing to monitor the response to worship, for instance, may not only improve its value for the congregation, but also lead to a willingness for others to subject their responsibilities to the loving scrutiny of others.

It is worth looking at Acts 20.17–38 in the light of the six roles I have mentioned. This passage is a summary of Paul's ministry among the Ephesians. To what extent does it show Paul fulfilling these roles? Are there other tasks which he performed which suggest other crucial roles for the central leader? Fill in table 7 to help you.

Warnings

Clearly, no one person is going to be equally and adequately competent in these six roles. What matters is that they are all carried

Table 7 **ACTS 20.17–38**

	Role	Verses	Main point
1.	Envisioner	27	Kingdom of God
2.	Teacher	20	Taught publicly and in homes
3.	Director	28	"Be shepherds"
4.	Facilitator	32	Building up via word
5.	Modeller	24,19–20	"Reckon own life worth nothing"
6.	Evaluator	21	"Gave warnings"
7.			
8.			
9.			

out, which involves a clear recognition by the church's, or the organization's, leaders that they are necessary. It is vital that the central leader involves others to strengthen them where he or she is less adequate. It is helpful if the central leaders give others the opportunity to share their evaluations of the central leaders' strengths and weakness (part of modelling!). It is also valuable if the central leaders share the roles where they are strong, because this will help others become strong in those areas too, and will often sharpen up the strengths of the leaders even more. If these roles are handled by a team, the team will need to share out the responsibilities clearly. It is important that skills in handling these roles go on developing. Clearly the facilitating role is vital for this process. There are many books and courses available for us today, and a good place to start is with the Marc Europe ones.

Tasks

○ × 1. Draw up a five year plan to review the life of your church or Christian organization. How will priorities be established? How will the people involved be consulted? How will the plan and its purpose be communicated to the church/organization and "the neighbourhood"? How will alterations of direction be implemented? How will the process be reviewed? How can flexibility be built into the process?

○ × 2. Consider an aspect of your organization's life, like the newsletter or organizational publication, the appointment of a youth organization leader, flower arranging for church or catering for the organization. (If possible choose an issue which is pertinent to your church or organization, but please ensure that the appropriate people know, and that all understand the level of the task — is it for real, or is it a training exercise?) Work out which issues need to be considered; how to examine fully, whilst minimizing any sense of criticism or threat to those involved; who needs to be consulted, and when; what facts need to be discovered, and how best to do this; how will the process and investigation be communicated etc. and who needs to know.

○ △ 3. For your church or group seek for God's vision. Prepare a plan on how you will share that vision with others. How you will check out it is God's vision. How you will move from a vision to a plan.

○ × 4. i) Talk with the central leaders. With their permission find out:
   a) What they did five years ago they are not doing now, and why.
   b) What they are doing now they think they really ought not to be doing, and why this is so.
   c) What they expect to do/not do in five year's time.
   d) What kind of leaders they will need to cover this.

   ii) Talk with them about the problems they face both with themselves and from other people in the transitions. Explore with them factors which might make the transition easier for themselves and for others.

   iii) With the central leader's permission write a confidential report summarizing the findings and seeking their confirmation, and making suggestions about future developments.

○ △ 5. If you are the central leader invite two or three people along and work from the other side. Explain you would like them to produce a report for you covering 4 iii) and provide them with a guidance sheet if required. Think through the purpose of such an exercise and, if feasible, meet with them again to see how together you can implement valuable insights gained. Afterwards list what auxiliary tasks have been fulfilled through this exercise.

○ ✕ 6. Draw a cartoon type picture to illustrate the changing role of the leader.

✕ 7. Devise a way, appropriate for your church or group, to find out what gifts, and the skills people have, and how this information can be available as a resource for the whole church or organization.

○ 8. Consider how, and to what extent, Jesus fulfilled the six higher roles. Are there other roles he fulfilled?

✕ 9. Consider how the six roles are carried out in your organization or church. Who has the responsibility for them? Evaluate the effectiveness of the roles. Either score each out of a maximum of 10, or list them in order.
What do you think your organization needs to do to improve its effectiveness? How can you help this happen? Will you monitor the results?

○ ✕ 10. Draw, or otherwise construct, a visual presentation of the six higher roles to show either what they involve, why they are necessary, or both.

○ 11. Design training exercises to develop skills for one or more of the higher roles. How and when will you try them out?

△ 12. Talk with your prayer partners about which of the six roles you should be moving into more strongly. Try to see what this means for you — personal development, spiritual gifts, training, opportunities. Agree to pray along these lines for a set period e.g. six months. Agree to monitor progress together after one month, three months, six months etc.

References — Chapter 9

1. Charles Sibthorpe, *A Man Under Authority* (Kingsway, 1984), p.235.
2. In contrast to P Beasley-Murray, *Dynamic Leadership* (Kingsway, 1990), p.128.
3. John Perry, *Effective Christian Leadership* (Hodder and Stoughton, 1983), p.98.
4. A useful chapter on this is Philip King, *Leadership Explosion* (Hodder and Stoughton, 1987), pp.136–140.
5. With apologies to E R Dayton and T W Engstom, *Strategy for Leadership* (Marc Europe, 1985), p.77.

6. Quoted by P Greenslade, *Leadership* (Marshalls Paperbacks, 1984), p.136.
7. A Le Peau, *Paths of Leadership* (IVP, 1984), p.90.
8. Cf. P Beasley-Murray, op.cit. p.27.
9. David Cormack, *Seconds Away* (Marc Europe, 1986), especially p.139.

CHAPTER 10

CARING FOR THE LEADER

> SUNDAY
> Got into one of those awful mental spins at church today. Felt depressed when I got there …
> MONDAY
> Not so much a quiet time as a silent, motionless time. Why am I so low? My spiritual life is in tatters.
> TUESDAY
> Anne demanded to know what was making me so irritable. Got really angry. I'm *not* irritable![1]

Goal

To enable people to develop appropriate motives and resources for Christian leadership and to be aware of their own position.

Aims

1. To highlight the kinds of pressure leadership brings.
2. To consider the significance of right motivation for the Christian leader.
3. To suggest proper ways of coping with these pressures by realizing God's resources, developing our use of these, and increasing our Christian concern for one another and our effectiveness in helping to protect the leader's person.

Main Scriptures

Matthew 23; 2 Corinthians 10–12; 1 Corinthians 13

Introduction

Caring for the leader includes caring for ourselves, if we are leading. Such caring is not self-centred but an essential part of our God-given task. Athletes who want to run 5,000 metres have to care for themselves, look after their diet, their hobbies, their relationships, their emotional and physical well-being etc. It is no good them saying "I will only run 5,000 metres". The other areas of living are integrated with their ability to perform. So for the Christian leader caring for ourselves, and being willing to receive that care from others, is integral to our involvement in leadership.

In Ephesians 6.10–18 Paul indicates the need for Christians to take appropriate steps to look after themselves spiritually (also 1 Timothy 4.6). Elsewhere he recommends that leaders look after themselves physically (1 Timothy 5.23) and relationally (1 Timothy 4.12). He is not averse to asking for help himself (2 Timothy 4.9–12) or to thanking those who cared for him (Philippians 4.10–18).

We also need to recognize our responsibility to care for those who lead us (Hebrews 13.17–18) and for those who lead for us (1 Peter 5.1–7). Caring for leaders, whether ourselves or others, means appreciating the pressures we are under, and then protecting ourselves sensibly and resourcing ourselves properly. Just as we recognize that those who work in the radiography unit of a hospital need to take special precautions over dress and procedures to avoid exposure to X-rays, so Christian leaders need to be aware of the risks in their situations and to take appropriate preventive and remedial actions.

Most of the risks for leaders arise out of the pressures which leadership brings. Two of the areas which we shall consider in more detail are those of motivation and energy drain. However, it is worth sketching in the sorts of pressures leadership generates, and as we read the following it is important to ask to what extent these pressures are affecting us, or those leaders we care for.

Growth situations bring additional pressures. Developing other people's leadership will change the leader's own role. Change always creates stress and, unless handled properly, leads to distress. Becoming an envisioner is riskier than a maintainer, and risk is a pressure. As soon as we develop into a team, communication and conflict become essential. Achieving good communication is a pressure, minimizing conflict is a pressure. Failure in either area generates far more! Deploying new leaders releases the main leader from some demands, but usually it is for more work and, normally, for more demanding tasks. A defeated and drained leader is not very effective and is little fun to be with, either for himself, his family or his friends. So it is to everyone's advantage to be aware of these pressures and to seek to help one another in a thoroughly Christian way. It is worth taking time out to think through the pressures we (or those we are responsible for) are coping with now in comparison with, say, three years ago, e.g. in family, work, leisure, church, and Christian service. Are these pressures greater, or more tolerable, or just different? Are we coping with more pressure better or not? Why?

It has always been an effective strategy for an enemy to capture or destroy the leaders. Satan is well aware of this. The destruction of leaders is always a prime target. In the temptations, he was seeking to destroy Jesus' leadership. Peter's attempt to deflect Jesus from the cross in Mark 8.31–33, was intended to be a double blow. If Peter had succeeded both Jesus and Peter would have fallen. In order to maintain his leadership Jesus had to risk his relationship with Peter. We need to be aware that leaders are prime targets for attack. Satan does not often destroy by killing but often by discrediting, demoralizing or dividing. For this, and other reasons, we need to pay special attention to our motives as Christian leaders.

Jesus drew special attention to the dangers of wrong motivation among the leaders of God's people. These are all the more dangerous when the leaders have reached the position where they are unclear about their own motivation. Chapter 23 of Matthew is a strong attack on religious leaders for hypocrisy — for not practising what they preach, but it is not hard to see that wrong motivation lies behind much of the "credibility gap". However, we must not accept every observation about our wrong motives as true. Jesus was accused of working for Beelzebub, for instance, and stoutly defended himself (Mark 3.20–30), but in fact the temptations show us he could easily have worked for Satan if he had not sorted out his ultimate allegiance (Matthew 4.8–10), and if he had not out-faced the real possibility of doing all he did for his own ego (Matthew 4.5–7). So, whilst people are likely to challenge us and criticize us in terms of our motives we should examine ourselves carefully, neither being destroyed by their comments, nor defensive about them.

Some of the wrong motives the Bible shows us are printed in table 8. Alongside them are two columns, one to list examples you have come across in others, the second to note occasions when you have been tempted by, or succumbed to, such motives. Please add other scriptural references that come to mind.

Table 8

Motive	Scriptures	Others	Self
Love of money	1 Timothy 6.9–10		
Pride	1 Timothy 3.6		
Ambition	Philippians 1.17		
Fear of others	1 Timothy 4.12		
Desire for approval	2 Corinthians 10.18[2]		
Sense of power	Acts 8.19		

I suggest that the list for others should become a challenge to repent for our brothers and sisters before God, and to pray for their restoration. The list for ourselves provides us with an opportunity to invite God to help us (probably we can involve our prayer partners too). Even when we think we can perceive wrong motives in other people we must be careful not to dismiss other people's Christian work. When good results are forthcoming we need to be very careful (Matthew 7.16–20). Paul delights in the success of others' preaching, even though they preach to make him jealous and because they envy his success (Philippians 1.15–18). Jesus warns us against criticizing others before we have thoroughly examined ourselves (Matthew 7.1–5). When there is a real team spirit so that we know we are truly loved, then we can help one another check out our motives. However, rather than become so introspective that we allow the possibility of some wrong motives deterring us from leading, we need to cultivate positive and valuable motives. Here are some scriptural ones:

A desire to help people	1 Corinthians 12.19, Romans 1.11–12
Love for God's people	1 Corinthians 14.1
Love for God	John 14.23
Obedience to God	John 15.10
Approval by God	2 Timothy 2.15
Fruitfulness	John 15.8
Praise and glory given to God	Matthew 5.16

It is a rare thing for anyone to do things from absolutely pure motives so, rather than having our motives completely right before we start, we need to be moving in the right direction. As we lead for God, Jesus through his Holy Spirit will be helping us (Galatians 5.16–26). Satan will equally be seeking to kidnap our motives and motivation by creating despondency, doubt, and double–mindedness. Confessing to one another can be a valuable defence, so can fasting, and so can living in a family. Each of these, in a different way, makes it more difficult to deceive ourselves about motivational factors.

There are also practical steps we can take to hinder the growth of wrong motives. When Jesus sent people out in pairs it was, perhaps, not only for their protection and mutual support, but also to limit pride in their individual achievement. As team leaders we need to take whatever practical steps we can to hinder the growth of wrong motivational forces and foster the positive ones. We shall also need to help others face the issue of wrong motives, and this makes it all the more essential that our own hearts are right before God. It is necessary that we make ourselves vulnerable by encouraging honest comment from others and by dealing with observations seriously, even if they are spoken in anger. There is many a truth spoken in jealousy as well as in jest.

We need to discover ways which are scriptural and practical to help others purify their motives and to restore them when they fall. It is vital that people feel upheld and respected by us (and God) throughout either of these processes (Galatians 6.1–5; John 21.15ff.). Although it is a leader's responsibility to help the growth of proper motivation, we are not ultimately responsible for other people (Galatians 6.5). They must make their own choices and sometimes, like Jesus, we shall "fail" to keep them (Jesus and Judas).

In Luke 4.14 we are told of Jesus "...the power of the Holy Spirit was with him". This comment follows the story of the temptations. Through those temptations Jesus was sorting out right and wrong motives. This process made the empowering of the Holy Spirit possible. Similarly, in John 4.34, Jesus can claim that obedience is like food. It provides him with the resources he needs. Hence sorting out our motives, hooking into godly ones, and jettisoning negative ones, can be a powerful "rocket boost" and is not an energy sapping diversion.

Many other factors besides our motives affect our energy level and to some of these we now turn. A Rolls Royce may be a splendid car to own but if there is no petrol or no power from the battery it won't go very far. Even if the battery was fully charged to start with, if it were not being recharged it would soon be powerless and the whole vehicle would stop. We can consider three basic kinds of energy level:

The Levels

1. Physical — otherwise our bodies don't function and the other levels of our being soon deteriorate.
2. Emotional — whether we are depressed or elated affects all our other processes.
3. Spiritual — our relationship with God is a vital source of energy.

But why does one person get fat and another person stay thin on the same number of calories? They use up energy at different rates. So we need to know what factors drain our energy, what storage capacity we have and how often we need to fill up. We need to make sure our alternator is supplying the battery with power as we go along. There are many ways of cataloguing the factors which drain our energy, and therefore cause us to need energy, but here is one simple categorization:

The Needs

1. The person we are
2. The people we interact with
3. The situations we cope with

For each category of our energy needs we can consider the three energy levels. Care is required in making proper assessment because exactly what is going on is not always obvious. For instance, we may be sitting in a deck chair in the garden with no problems and no-one to bother us, but if we are engaged in spiritual warfare the energy drain can be enormous.

The Person we are

At each level — physical, emotional, and spiritual — we need to know what kind of person we are. We need to know whether we are generally well-resourced or weak at any level. We need to know what particular things are likely to have a large effect on us. For instance, I am basically fit and strong but certain physical tasks affect my back and the consequent pain has a large effect on my resources. Someone else may have large emotional resources but find that there are certain issues which drain them rapidly. We need to know whether we require to replenish our energy levels frequently, and in small amounts, or in larger quantities and less frequently. We need to know what sort of "food" suits us best. Then we need to look after our energy needs unashamedly unless we are really prevented from so doing. As leaders we need to help others do the same. As leaders we need to let others help us, whilst recognizing that the normal may not suit us best.

Some of the major factors we should consider for our personal energy levels:

1. Physical — exercise, rest and sleep, food and drink.
2. Emotional — security, relaxation, social contacts, mental stimulation, hobbies.
3. Spiritual — renewal e.g. confession, study, reading, vision, fellowship; exercises e.g. prayer, Bible study, Bible meditation, singing, worship; relationship with God e.g. openness, consistency, enjoyment.

The People with Whom we Interact

People have a profound effect on our energy level, just like the kind of load a vehicle carries affects its performance and energy requirements. If we live with, work with, and play with, energy sapping people we shall require plenty of energy input. So we need to be aware of the effect on us of people around us. If we live on our own then we have special demands to cope with, but we have more control over the choice of people with whom we associate in our "free" time. But people living on their own may still have family commitments which can be demanding. If we live in a family or other community then the other members have a profound effect on us. One of the more difficult factors to manage is the change in demands which the family brings. We can, and should, keep a family diary of predictable events so we can attempt not to overload ourselves when family demands will be high. But this is not always successful. Other people and their situations are not always under our control. We cannot determine when someone will have an accident or die. Committees will decide to meet at our most inconvenient time.

Conversely, my experience is that the unpredictable family demands occur in clusters, just when other pressures are greatest. One of the children catches chicken pox, or an emotional crisis arises so that someone needs a lot of personal support, just at the time when everyone else needs us desperately. It is as though Satan knows when and where we are most vulnerable! There are some strategies we can use to cope with these factors:

1. The better the quality of our normal relationships in the family, the more understanding the members will be, even if they think you should be making them more of a priority. Praying, playing, sharing together regularly will help everyone cope better with the unpredictable pressures.
2. Some people will want always to have a "safety margin" in their commitment level, some will need to let their partner check their diary. Some will provide this "safety margin" by including in their commitments longer term projects which can act like shock absorbers, levelling out the ups and downs of demand.
3. Whatever strategy we use we should ensure that it is not always our family we put second or third or… Sometimes they should come first. When we put others first, we should explain why.
4. As a member of a family we need to be aware that any pressure (however reasonable and necessary) we put on others will be felt especially keenly. So, often the best time to sort things out is not when the pressures are already great, or when we are already feeling neglected. Neither must issues be avoided or resentment allowed to fester. So an agreed review time, every month or three months, can be a valuable way to cope.
5. Finally, remember that God has promised not to allow us to be tempted beyond our limits. There is a proper exit, or escape route available. So we don't need to feel sorry for ourselves, or panic. Rather we need to look for his solution.

But it is good to recall that people, including our families, can also supply us with energy, they can be filling stations. So we need to know which people suit us best.

Again we can consider the impact of people on us at our three levels:

1. Physical — If we spend our day lifting elderly people or running a club for ten year olds we can expect to be drained physically. Equally, physical exercise with people could replenish our energy level. Or people we lead can do physically draining tasks for us.
2. Emotional — This is probably the most significant energy drain and resourcing level in the people category. A helpful book for understanding this process is Gordon MacDonald's *Restoring Your Spiritual Passion* (Highland, 1987). A summary of its argument is given in Appendix A. We need to understand how people affect us emotionally. At times of extra demand we need

to gather resourcing people around us. Working through this book drains energy, hence prayer partners are important. Most people will welcome the opportunity to resource us emotionally. Many of them, perhaps surprisingly, will find that doing so energizes, rather than drains, them. So please don't be afraid to involve those who can help you. They will often be people you like, whom you feel understand you, and with whom you feel comfortable.

3. Spiritual — Some people make God and his purposes more real for us. Some distort our vision, deflect our commitment and drain us spiritually. Jesus is the supreme example of the former, those who are demon possessed are likely to have the strongest negative spiritual effects. Most people will be in between! If we have a close and positive relationship with someone, they will resource us. If we sense tension or antagonism they will drain us. We can't be resourced by people we keep at a distance; we will be drained by people who dominate us. A significant factor as to how people affect us is how we relate to them.

The Situations

Town driving requires more energy per mile than steady motorway driving. Ascending requires more than descending (although too much of this can wear out the brakes). Similarly, the situations in which we are functioning affect our energy levels.

1. Physical — Some situations are physically demanding. For instance, very hot or very cold conditions, or trekking through the jungle to take the gospel, or house to house visitation in the urban jungle. Some are physically restoring: a pleasant spring day or sitting in front of a warm fire in a comfortable armchair, with coffee and cream cakes, are illustrations of this!
2. Emotional — Coping with stressful crises, or working with a boring routine are emotionally draining, whilst achieving objectives and solving problems tend to be emotionally energizing.
3. Spiritual — Some situations soak up our energy. Working in a pagan or anti-Christian environment will take its toll on us. Conversely, doing Christian things with Christian people can energize us. What better than to write a Christian book!

Hopefully this brief analysis will prompt us to start assessing what is happening to our energy level. It may even give us clues as to why we become tired, depressed or ineffective. But there are some other salient points to incorporate into our evaluation. There are no absolute boundaries between these three levels. One factor will influence another so we need to be properly resourced at all three levels. Normally we need to be resourced physically as well as spiritually. However, it is well worth being aware that things from one level can restore us in another. For instance, after an emotionally draining hospital visit to a terminally ill patient we might be restored by buying and enjoying a chocolate bar. If we are feeling emotionally depressed, playing a Christian tape, either a teaching or worship tape, may well compensate for our emotional emptiness.

We can also be over-resourced. A full tank of petrol in a racing car is a disadvantage in terms of its performance. Having lots of fat is a physical source of energy, but it is not a good thing to carry excess. Spiritually, we can take in too much and become clogged up. Efficiency means carrying only sufficient resources, but we need to carry enough for the long journeys! Planning our energy needs is important (cf. 1 Kings 19.4–9).

What resources one person may drain another. So, as leaders, we need to use people, including ourselves, as far as possible in ways that resource each individual rather than drain each individual. People need to operate as themselves i.e. using their own natural and spiritual gifts, normally operating within their own leadership styles, working close to people with whom they feel comfortable and who do not cause them conflict etc.

Our ultimate aim is not self-preservation but Christian service. There are times when it is right to become exhausted in Christian service. Again, the ultimate example is Jesus dying on the cross. He was exhausted of supplies physically, emotionally, and spiritually. The resurrection shows that God will take care of us even in those situations. Normally, however, it is right to resource ourselves adequately. "Be kind to one another, tender hearted…" This includes being kind to our own self.

We have a responsibility to resource ourselves and, as leaders, to ensure that those for whom we are responsible are resourced too. Hence we need to know ourselves, and those we lead, well. It may well be helpful to fill in the two charts, tables 9 and 10, which follow and if you are leading others to help them do the same. Please note down in the boxes factors which influence you. It may be helpful to review these each day for a fortnight.

Filling in the table won't help by itself. We need to apply our insights. So we need to use our awareness to minimize draining of resources by avoiding danger zones and by balancing, building up reserves etc. when we foresee danger. Remember, in general we

Table 9
A **ENERGY GAIN**

	Person Who I am	**Interaction** How people help me	**Situation** What stimulates and comforts me
Physical			
Emotional			
Spiritual			

Table 10
B **ENERGY LOSS**

	Person Who I am	**Interaction** Who drains me	**Situation** What tires me etc.
Physical			
Emotional			
Spiritual			

shall drain others unless we are adequately resourced but we must be willing to surrender our resources for Christ's sake. If we benefit from being led God calls us to do everything we can to resource our leaders (cf. Philippians 2.25–29; 1 Timothy 5.17–18), do please give leaders the freedom to let you know what really helps. It is wonderful that people pass to me "helpful" books, but when I have twenty waiting to be read it can become quite a drain! Besides knowing our motives and what resources us, we need also to face, realistically, the price and privileges of leadership. To this we now turn.

Tasks

○△ 1. Describe situations to show where and how unhelpful motives could develop in your life. Ask God (personal prayer), your spouse, and children, or your prayer partners to help you examine your motives. It is hard not to become defensive so here are two suggestions to help:
   i) Each person is given a list of ulterior motives and is asked to note down when they suspect these operate in your life. Then each person can speak for five minutes about your motivation. *You are committed to silence.* At the end you are given their piece of paper to pray through.
   ii) Each prayer partner is asked to write a letter seeking to share with you their insights into your motivation.

   Debriefing is very important for this exercise. Each of us will need the support from others to cope with comments made, and a plan to replace ulterior motives with positive ones. We shall need our prayer partners for this.

○△ 2. Make a list of the qualities of love in 1 Corinthians 13.4–7. Beside the list draw five columns. Think prayerfully through the last seven days. Give yourself a tick for every occasion you expressed any quality of love and a cross every time you failed. Decide from this which aspect of love needs most attention. Ask for the Holy Spirit to be poured into your heart to give you God's love (Romans 5.5; Luke 11.9–13) every day for a fortnight. Draw up another list of 1 Corinthians 13.4–7 and every day throughout the period review daily with ticks and crosses. Obviously prayer partners will be a great support in this process.

○ ✕ 3. Look at three leadership roles in your church (preferably at different levels of leadership. What is the potential for wrong motivation? How could things be arranged practically to avoid wrong motivation? e.g. counting the offering: have two people to avoid the love of money leading to theft. Flower arranging, danger of pride and/or jealousy: keep list of those doing arranging secret.

○ ✕ 4. If you suspect someone of unhelpful motives what can you do to help them and restore them? e.g. prayer, confrontation, change of roles. Should you do this on your own? If not what should govern the choice of person(s) with whom to share your concern? Think through scriptural principles and practical applications.

○ ✕ 5. Arrange a social and games evening for your leaders. Ask someone to observe how people behave in competitive situations. Then discuss this together. Alternatively, use games, quite openly, as a means of bringing out people's motives e.g. choose games which bring out bad or good motives. Let the participants discuss what they saw and felt.

References — Chapter 10

1. Adrian Plass, *The 1989 Sacred Diary* (Marshall Pickering, 1988).
2. The whole section, 2 Corinthians 10—12, shows the damage that leaders with wrong motivation can do to the church. It also shows how hard wrong motives can be to reveal and eradicate. A study of the passage with D A Carson, *From Triumphalism to Maturity* (IVP, 1986) is worthwhile.

CHAPTER 11

THE PEARL OF GREAT PRICE

There are however many legitimate benefits which we should accept as part of the loving kindness of God '...recognition... advancement... freedom... personal growth... fun.'[1]

"It all comes, I suppose", he decided, as he said good-bye to the last branch, spun round three times, and flew gracefully into a gorse bush, "It all comes of liking *honey so much."*[2]

Goal

To help people be realistic about the costs and rewards of Christian leadership.

Aims

1. To understand the costs of leadership through scriptural insight and through the lives of Christian leaders in order to:
   i) help us appreciate what our leaders are giving and learn how we can support them more effectively.
   ii) help us be honest with ourselves (and those we are encouraging into leadership) in facing the demands of leadership.
2. i) To identify the legitimate joys of leadership.
   ii) To learn how to maximize those joys for leaders, learners, and led.

Main Scriptures

Philippians 3.5–14; Acts 20.36–38; Philippians 1.3–8; Revelation 2—3.

Introduction

Canst thou, O partial sleep give thy repose
To the wet sea-boy in an hour so rude,
And in the calmest and most stillest night,
With all appliances and means to boot,
Deny it to a king? Then happy low, lie down
Uneasy lies the head that wears a crown.
(Henry IV Part II, Act 3 Scene 1, lines 26–31)

According to Shakespeare it's tough at the top. Why then are people usually clamouring and clambering over one another to get to the top? Part of the answer, and one which we as Christians can easily overlook, is that there can be tremendous rewards.

Living in Coventry in May 1987 was a tremendous experience. Coventry City football team won the FA Cup. That evening, as the fans returned home, the whole city became alive and fun to live in. People hooted and waved from their cars as they drove around. People who did not know one another smiled and talked. It felt as though we had won a war! So a city which was struggling with unemployment and depression, bathed for a few days in glory and victory. As the team returned on the Sunday, the streets were full of happy, cheering, fulfilled people. The team — the players, coach, and manager — were heroes. There were, of course, great rewards for them: success, fame, finance etc. and some of their joys were consciously transferred to the whole city. Enjoyment of victory helps leaders and followers to keep going when defeat happens and playing or supporting seems hard work.

Is this one reason why churches have special festive occasions, or why marriage begins with a wedding day? We shall come back to these rewards, but it is valuable for leaders and followers to be realistic about the price of Christian leadership. Jesus' parable about the pearl, points out that it is only obtainable by those who are willing to sacrifice everything to get it (Matthew 13.45–46).

The Price of Leadership

Many of the greatest leaders have been very honest about the cost of following them.

Garibaldi: "I promise you forced marches, short rations, bloody battles, wounds, imprisonment, and death..."[3]

Churchill: "I have nothing to offer but blood, toil, tears and sweat."[4]

This is also true for Jesus. Matthew chapter 10 gives us a sample of this honesty.

"Listen! I am sending you out just like sheep to a pack of wolves. You must be as cautious as snakes and as gentle as doves." (Matthew 10.16)

"No pupil is greater than his teacher; no slave is greater than his master. ...if the head of the family is called Beelzebul, the members of the family will be called even worse names!" (Matthew 10.24, 25)

"A man's worst enemies will be the members of his own family." (Matthew 10.36)

"Whoever does not take up his cross and follow in my steps is not fit to be my disciple." (Matthew 10.38)

People who can afford to say this kind of thing to their followers have already examined realistically the cost of leadership and the significance of their cause. They have also decided that the rewards outstrip the costs. Such leaders are in a strong position for they can share honestly the costs of following where they are leading, knowing the "pearl" is worth it to them, and to any followers worth having with them. So every leader needs to be ruthlessly honest about the price they are willing to pay. This frees them to be honest with their followers and frees their followers to be supportive to their leaders if, and when, the going gets tough.

So let's return to Jesus. Jesus knew he would end up crucified, and he warned his disciples that crucifixion was the price of following him. He also knew there were great rewards which made the agony worthwhile (Hebrews 12.2). It was this knowledge which enabled him to share the reality of being cross-bearers with his disciples. He allowed them to leave but some, at least, chose to stay.

But ending up on a cross was not the total price Christ paid for being the leader he was. Many other problems come crowding into our minds: bitter opposition from the religious and political leaders; coping with his disciples — their squabbles, lack of faith, incompetence, and mistakes; the vacillation of the crowds — first their clamour and ceaseless demands, then their cowardly and thoughtless rejection; the misunderstanding and hurts from his human family; no secure home of his own; loneliness; weariness... The list could easily be extended, not only for Jesus but for almost any leader who is presented in Scripture. It is worth reviewing the biblical leaders we have studied and noting the costs they incurred. It is also worth asking ourselves what joys did they have and would they have made it easier for others to follow them and support them if they had spelled out the cost?

It is equally valid to think through the demands made on contemporary Christian leaders, whether that be Billy Graham or Bishop Tutu, Mother Theresa or Jackie Pullinger. Lack of privacy, criticism, danger, misrepresentation, hero-worship, tiredness, frustration would probably be some. The closer we come to such people in our understanding the more puzzling the questions: Why do they put up with it? Do they have no choice? Are they in some way perverted? They don't seem to be such people. Are they, in fact, being resourced by rewards which make it all worthwhile? Before we consider this more carefully there are a few issues to note first.

It is important to keep these matters in perspective. Jesus had some good times too. He went to parties, sailed on the lake, had meals prepared for him, was cheered by the friendship and insight of the disciples etc. Secular leaders at all levels also pay a price for their leadership so we, with our extra resources from God, should not be too soft on ourselves. Here in the West our "price tag" is much less than for other Christians in Central America, China, Uganda or Eastern Europe, and our lot is much easier than it has been for many through Christian history. We are, in fact, often unknowingly the beneficiaries of their sacrifice and should be challenged by this. As Hebrews 12.1 reminds us: "As for us, we have this large crowd of witnesses round us... let us run with determination the race that lies before us."

A review of biblical leaders (and some contemporary ones) also shows that some end up paying a higher price for leadership than they need (David, Samson, Peter), because of their disobedience and their apparent inability to heed God's directives. We need to watch this constantly. But we can also make the demands of leading higher than necessary by neglecting, or refusing, the resources that God provides for us to make our load lighter. The man who carries the donkey and its load has rather missed the point! God gives leaders the resources they need. Here, too, he provides the escape route. Throughout this book we have been concerned to show that other people and prayer are God's resources for us.

In the early days of my ministry in my present church I began to feel burdened by the serious responsibility of leadership. The church felt like a weight I was carrying. Once I realized that it was God's church, and that his people should be sharing the burden, the weight lifted. Although I still felt responsible I was now much freer to cope properly. A key factor in this change was organizaing prayer support for my ministry. Something, of course, which Paul was always doing! If we do not use God's resources then we run into another danger, that of projecting our costs onto others, or expressing our costs to others. We can do this not only with the real demands, but also with exaggerated or imaginary ones. We can bathe in people's admiration or enjoy seeing them squirm under the pressures we project. Such a way of leading is clearly wrong, is usually unnecessary, and will be counter-productive, driving people from us and making them fearful of supporting us. Anyway, if others share the cost of our leadership, they should do so voluntarily.

If we are going to avoid such unhelpful procedures, if we are going to recognize our need of God's resources and if we are going to be free to share the price of following with others, then we need to look honestly at the cost of our present leadership and learn how to evaluate that cost for the future. I find the following consideration helpful: *What does my leadership cost me?*

Time How much time do I give and what does this mean I no longer do which I would like to do?

Stress What tensions do I have to cope with because I am leading? Do I enjoy these and find them stimulating, or are they wearing me down?

Frustration Because I lead I am personally committed to the project: difficulties and hold-ups I therefore experience as painful.

Isolation Because I am leading I am less one of the crowd. How much does this really matter to me?

Rejection Often this is too strong a word, but do I now feel I am sitting on opposite sides to people with whom I formerly sat side by side?

Pressures Because I am a leader I become a target. Do I sense

that Satan is putting me under pressure to compromise, be proud, do wrong etc? Are there others who are also "shooting" at me?
Finance Am I involved in loss of earnings, or do I contribute financially to the project because of my commitment to it?
Risk I could avoid the risk of mistakes, criticism, and failure by having no goals, targets of achievements, but then there would be no real success. What effect does living with risk have on me?
Others We can specify our own.
What does my leadership cost others? Particularly as Christians it is important we consider the ways our leadership affects other people, especially those close to us, including our family, friends, work colleagues, those above us and below us, our neighbours. Inevitably, if we accept leadership roles, we shall have less time to socialize or build contacts for Christian witness. As Christian leaders we need constantly to work at minimizing the detrimental effect of our position on others. For instance, Jesus, knowing the cross was imminent, tried to prepare his disciples (John 14—16), he prayed for them intensely (John 17; Luke 22.31–32), he handed his mother over to John for him to care for (John 19.26). After his crucifixion he also found ways to use the negative effects of his death to help others (John 20.24–20; 21.15–19).

I have found the following steps helpful in reducing the cost of my leadership on other people:
Check Am I doing God's work? Am I doing it his way? Am I accepting all the resources he is making available?
Involve When making decisions to take on extra responsibilities, I try to include people who are likely to be affected in the decision making process. This may mean I share the opportunity with them, pray with them and involve them, at an appropriate level, in the decision, or even surrender the decision to them. They then find it easier to cope because the outcome is partly their choice, and not something arbitrarily imposed on them.
Ask I ask people to monitor the impact of my leadership on them and to discuss with me ways of adjusting any detrimental effects. Often other people are more aware than we are, both of the effects and the most helpful ways of making adjustments for them.

The Pearl of Leadership

In order to become the great Christian leader he was Paul gave up a great deal (Philippians 3.5–7) and put up with even more (2

Corinthians 11.16–33), yet he had no hesitations: the benefits far outweigh the costs (Philippians 3.7,14). According to Hebrews, the same is true for Moses (11.24–26). "...he kept his eyes on the future reward". Jesus too, whilst he warned of the costs, also promised rewards which completely outshone the costs (Matthew 19.27–29).

Whilst there are rewards which are inappropriate for Christian leaders to seek, and even proper rewards which should not be pursued inappropriately, there are valid and significant benefits which come to every Christian leader, and which God wants us to enjoy. It is worth returning to Acts 20 again and Paul's farewell to the Ephesian elders.

> *When Paul finished, he knelt down with them and prayed. They were all crying as they hugged him and kissed him good-bye. They were especially sad because he had said that they would never see him again. And so they went with him to the ship. (Acts 20.36–38)*

Here are some of our rewards: spiritual companionship, affection, emotional support. And behind these lie many more: conversion and growth, development of loyal leaders and co-workers, fulfilment of God-given tasks. As Paul, echoing Jesus, said "There is more happiness in giving than in receiving".

God wants us to enjoy the rewards of our leadership. I made a note of some of the joys of leadership which I find personally enriching and which, I believe, are scripturally valid.

1. Approval and affirmation from God (often we experience this through his people).
2. Achievement of worthwhile tasks with eternal significance.
3. Personal maturation of people in Christ.
4. Upbuilding of the Christian community.
5. Loyalty, love, and friendship from those I seek to serve.
6. Personal growth and enrichment.

I think it is helpful for us to look at our own lives and note the rewards we like. What lifts us, satisfies us, pleases us, brings us joy. Note what rewards we receive. Then we need to confirm that they are legitimate scripturally. We must ensure that we only take what God permits. If we do receive what God offers we shall be less likely to look for those which he doesn't! However, please don't panic if, at first sight, your list of rewards doesn't appear to tally with Scripture. God is very generous and gives us everything for our enjoyment (1 Timothy 6.17). He loves to bless us in all kinds of ways that fit us personally, so please, if in any doubt, talk through your list with a trusted Christian friend. They may well be able to show you that your joys are right and proper. Even finance is a proper Christian reward (1 Timothy 5.17; Galatians 6.6).

Occasionally, we may discover either we are seeking a reward which is not from God, or taking it the wrong way. Then we must come to terms with God about this. But it may also be we haven't learnt to receive graciously what God offers and, as a result, we and others will be impoverished. Whilst I have stressed the need for leaders not to burden others with their costs, it is even more important that we do bless them with our joys. We need to give them positive feedback. Not only by thanking them and encouraging them, but by letting them see the joys we have. Often, of course, they will be the source of our joy. Many who work with us invest a great deal of themselves in us and for us in the service of God. Paul did not try to keep others at a distance, nor did Jesus. By sharing with them our enjoyment of leading we are teaching them the rightness of proper rewards and recognizing that this is one way God resources us.

We can see how integrated with God's people his rewards are and how Paul lets others know this, as we look at some verses from his letter to the Philippians.

> *I thank my God for you every time I think of you; and every time I pray for you all, I pray with joy because of the way in which you have helped me in the work of the gospel from the very first day until now. And so I am sure that God, who began this good work in you, will carry it on until it is finished on the Day of Christ Jesus. You are always in my heart! And so it is only right for me to feel as I do about you. For you have all shared with me in this privilege that God has given me, both now that I am in prison and also while I was free to defend the gospel and establish it firmly. God is my witness and I am telling the truth when I say that my deep feeling for you all comes from the heart of Christ Jesus himself.*

> *So then, my brothers, how dear you are to me and how I miss you! How happy you make me, and how proud I am of you! This then, dear brothers, is how you should stand firm in your life in the Lord.*

> *In my life in union with the Lord it is a great joy to me that after so long a time you once more had the chance of showing that you care for me. I don't mean that you had stopped caring for me — you just had no chance to show it.*
>
> *Here, then, is my receipt for everything you have given me — and it has been more than enough! I have all I need now that Epaphroditus has brought me all your gifts. They are like a sweet-smelling offering to God, a sacrifice which is acceptable and pleasing to him. (Philippians 1.3–8; 4.1,10,18)*

Paul exhibits a wonderful gift for expressing his own joys and simultaneously affirming other people. These verses read like a celebration of his ministry at Philippi. Such celebration, taking time out with others to enjoy each other, and our achievements with each other for God, doesn't come easily to me. Although I find it natural to say thank you and express appreciation, and although I love people deeply, I am also very task orientated. I find so much joy in seeing the task completed that I do not need to stop and celebrate with others. Achievements fire me up for the next task. But many people can stop and celebrate and enjoy their appropriate joys, so people like myself need to be careful not to be like the elder brother. We need to let others be blessed by our joys (Luke 15.25–32). Conversely, we need to share gladly in other people's joys. After all, God took time to enjoy his own creation (Genesis 1.10,12,18,25,31; 2.1–4), and he will spend all eternity with us celebrating his new creation.

Tasks

○✕ 1. Draw a diagram to illustrate the effect on your life, and others', of a new responsibility taking five hours a week. Give options and suggest how to compensate for disadvantages. An illustration is on page 165.

△ 2. You need someone else to take over one of your responsibilities (it might be the washing up, or it might be preaching once a Sunday etc). Think through how you can help them face the cost realistically, be equipped for the task, and experience your support. How do you avoid projecting your costs onto them?

○✕ 3. You are asked by the person above you in leadership to

Option 1

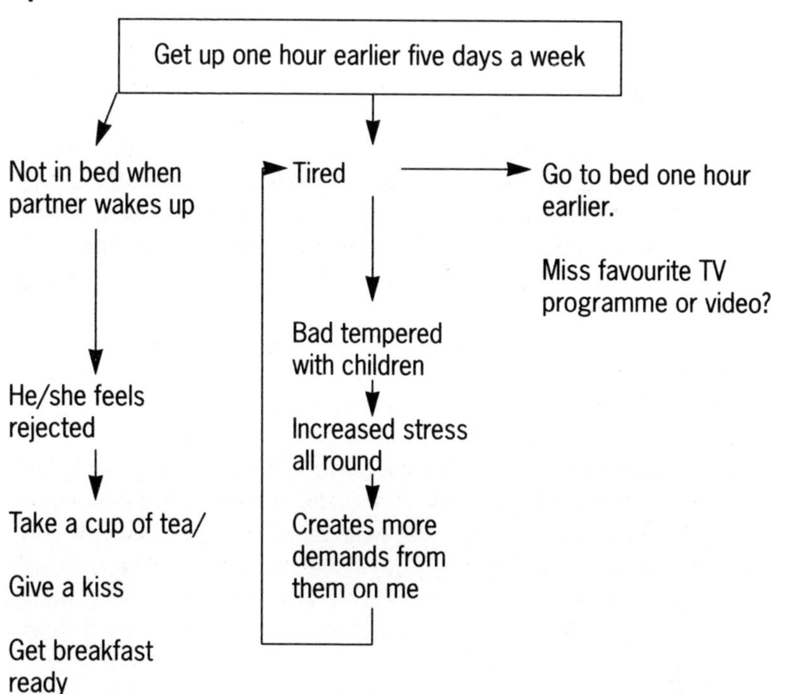

Option 2

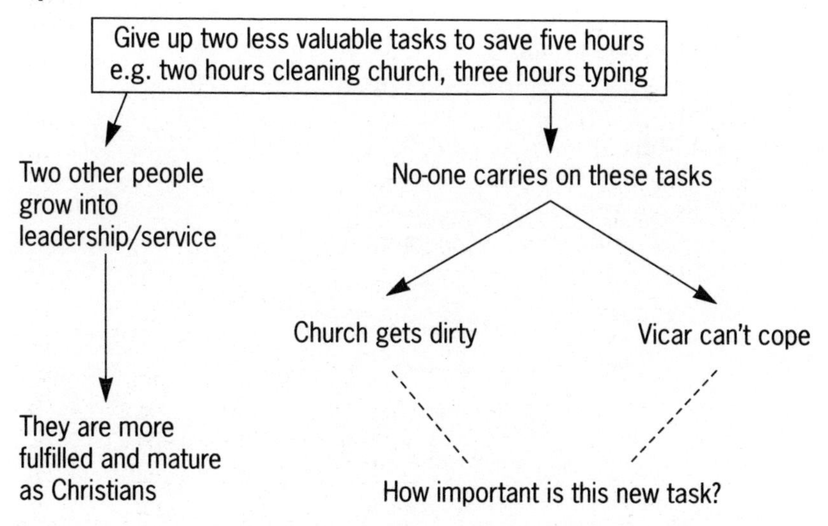

take on an additional responsibility. What questions do you need to ask them in order to calculate the costs and prepare yourself for the task? How can you minimize the effects on yourself? How can you minimize the effects on others (colleagues, team, family)?

△ 4. What have you gained from, and enjoyed about, this book? Can you find a way of sharing that with others? If you have prayer partners find a way of sharing your joys. If you have worked as a group why not plan a celebration — party? outing? Chinese take-away? a book burning ceremony?!

○ ✕ 5. Review the costs of using this book on time, energy etc. Is it cost effective? If not how can you gain more from it now you have made your investment? (See Conclusion for suggestions).

○ △ 6. Write a letter of appreciation to someone who has helped you grow in the past — Sunday school teacher, parent, Brigade officer, training manager etc., or more recently — prayer partners, leader or members of this group, or the author of the book! Share with them how they helped you, how this has been significant, and what you are doing with what they gave you.

○ ✕ 7. Make a brief list of, say, five costs to God of our redemption and five rewards. Why is God still committed to it? (Remember Colossians 1.19–23).

References — Chapter 11

1. John Finney, *Understanding Leadership* (Daybreak, 1989), p.188.
2. A A Milne, *Winnie the Pooh* (The Chaucer Press, 1966), p.7
3. Quoted by H E Fosdick, *The Manhood of the Master* (Student Christian Movement, 1914), p.48.
4. Speech to the House of Commons, 13 May 1940.

CONCLUSION

THE DOOR AND THE HOUSE

> *"If the Lord does not build the house, the work of the builders is useless..." (Psalm 127.1)*

Goal

To help the readers assess what they have gained from this book and to prepare them for future developments.

Aims

1. To review the content of this book.
2. To evaluate what has been learnt.
3. To consider possible "next steps".
4. To part as friends.

Main Scriptures

2 Timothy 2.3–7

Introduction

I would like you to imagine that you have left your house and just closed the door behind you. How do you feel? Does the door cut you off from the place you love and in which you feel secure? Are you sad to be leaving the family behind you? Or does the closing of the door mean freedom? You are on your way to an adventure? How we feel will depend on many factors. The kind of person we are will have a great influence on our immediate feelings. Whether we have rushed out after a brief return, or whether we have been in the house for days on end. What we are going off to do, how soon we will be coming back? How do we happen to be feeling on that day? Some are long term factors, some are short term.

The House

Now I would like you to imagine that you are going to meet up with a friend and they will say to you "What's your house like?" So as you close the door your mind tries to recapture what your house is like. Again, what comes to mind varies according to the person you are (an architect, an electrician, an interior designer, a housewife, a gardener; each would focus on different aspects), the person you will be talking to and, of course, the house itself. Most of us could give some account of the house because we would organize it into rooms which have functions and which bear relationships to one another (beside, above or below) but also because the person we are explaining it to has a somewhat similar house. Having organized our explanation into rooms we could begin to recall some of the details. It is just possible, if you are like me, that when you close that door and try to imagine it your mind goes blank or you can only think of another house. (This might especially be the case if I had been viewing several houses with the intention of purchasing one and the person I have to describe it to is my wife!)

The Rooms

As we come to the end of this book it is like leaving a house. In a moment of panic you might find it difficult to remember anything in the book! But pause, try and relate it to other books, i.e. it has chapters (like a house has rooms). How are the chapters related to one another etc. and see if you can write down the chapter heading, or a brief description in the house diagram overleaf. There are thirteen chapters (including the introduction and conclusion) so this house has thirteen rooms including the hall/stairway. Let's call this conclusion the exit/entrance lobby.

Then having given a name/description to each room you can perhaps go on to include some important points (that is important for you, or the kind of thing your friend would be interested in), very much as your mind might recapture some of the main items of furniture etc. in a room. It may be if yours is a family home, your home means people more than things — Martin programs (!) his computer here, Ann plays the piano, that's where Hannah has her dolls, and Steven cleans his football boots! So that for each room in the book you recall someone's struggle or excitement over it!

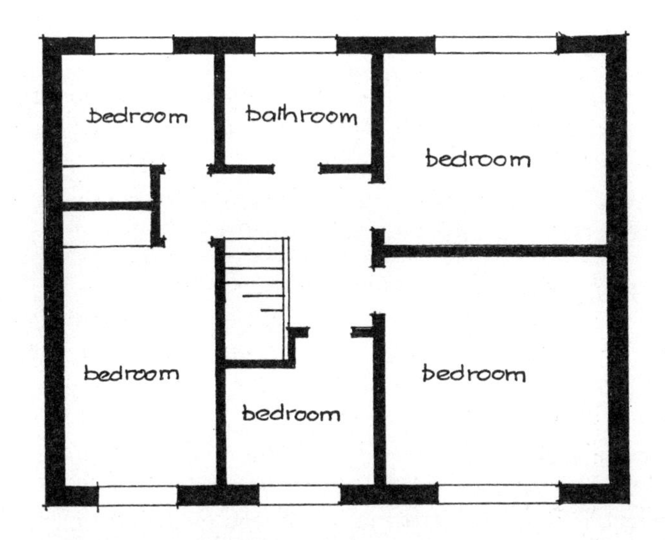

First Floor Plan.

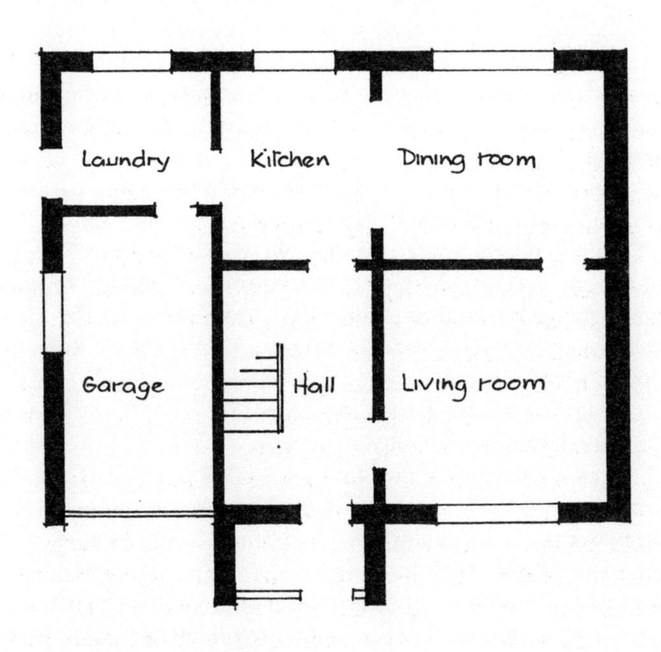

Ground Floor Plan.

But suppose you can't remember very much. What then? Well, you have the key to the house don't you? You can go back in and make notes and diagrams. You can even use the goal and aims for each chapter to help you recall what you have read. However, it's worth giving yourself half an hour before looking back because everyone who has read this book, and especially those who have worked at the tasks, will have learnt a lot about leading.

The Favourite

Most of us have favourite rooms. Perhaps because of the décor, or the view, or because we spend a lot of time there, or because of what happens there. Which is/are your favourite room(s) in this book and do you know why? Our favourite room may not be the most important from other people's point of view. To most people in a family the kitchen is probably the most important room, although it is not the favourite for all who prepare the meals and wash up! So is there a room which you recognize to be important for others because of what you can do through it — which chapter has challenged you most, or changed you most, or do you think will be most helpful for your serving? Please remember you can revisit the rooms as often as you wish so long as you have the book. In fact you may need to do that because at various points you skipped through a room (e.g. chapter 6). Or you may have been surveying the book by reading it and now want to return to consider it more seriously — like returning to view again the house you think you might buy.

However attractive a house might seem we need to ask the question "Can I afford it?" Nearly always we will sense "No, I can't", but if it's the house we want we will try hard to bridge the gap. So, can you afford to reuse this book? Can you afford not to? If you managed to find five hours extra time in the task at the end of the last chapter then clearly you can afford to do so. Remember the three ways of using the book (see page 6):

1. Read it and work at the tasks alone
2. Read it but involve prayer partners
3. Read it and share it in a group

The effect on your leadership potential will be far more marked if you rework the book at a higher level. Can you use your extra five hours more effectively?

But what if you have already used it at level three? Then if you led, your next step might be to support another person in leading the course for another group of leaders, and if you have been a member of such a group then your next step might be to lead the group. At whatever level you have used this book you are ready to work out a plan showing what steps you will need to take if you are going to reuse this book and gain even more. When will you work out your plan? At least decide this now. If you sense you need to rework this book then work hard at finding your five hours. This will not only give you the space but will also help you evaluate your priorities. If you can't plan it now, plan it for later.

The Adventure

But for the moment the door is closed and we are off. Each of us is off for something different. What are we called by God to be and do? We have said "the best Christian leader we can be". This will mean different things for all of us, but throughout our day the home we have left will be resourcing us and helping us, although most of the time we will be, quite properly, unaware of this. Throughout the day we shall need to supplement our home's resourcing — another meal, another wash, another quiet rest, another sit down, another read etc. I hope that the various appendices will help you select the appropriate additional resources you might need for the next stage in your journey of growing in Christian leadership.

It has been a real delight to write this book, not least because of the sense that through it God will be helping to build his people to do his work. So thank you for all the time and energy you have given in using this book. We may never meet on earth but we have become co-workers with Christ. So thank you. May I leave you with some words that another Christian writer sent to someone whose leadership potential he valued enormously?

> *Take your part in suffering, as a loyal soldier of Christ Jesus. A soldier on active service wants to please his commanding officer and so does not get mixed up in the affairs of civilian life. An athlete who runs in a race cannot win the prize unless he obeys the rules. The farmer who has done the hard work should have the first share of the harvest. Think about what I am saying, because the Lord will enable you to understand it all. (2 Timothy 2.3–7)*

Please pause and pray, asking God what this passage says to you.

Perhaps also giving thanks for things you have learnt from this book, people who have shared it in any way, for your leadership, for your church that it may grow as God wants.

Tasks

△ 1. Work out what God wants you to do with what you have gained through this course. You may need to talk with your leader (see Task 3) or with your prayer partners, or in your group. Decide when and how you will make the necessary arrangements.

○ 2. If you have not already done so use the house plan to review what you have gained from this book. You can either use each room for a chapter arbitrarily or you can use other factors as you wish e.g. size of room — size of chapter, function of room — function of chapter, relationship of issues to one another etc. If you wish you could furnish each room using main points for different pieces of furniture. Remember if you don't wish to spoil your book, or if you want more space to write, copy it or enlarge it. If you prefer draw your own house plan which is more appropriate to the way you see the book.

○× 3. Choose a date, three months or six months hence, and write a note in your diary that you will look again at this book and see what you remember, what you have been able to put into practice, what you need to refresh yourself about. Remember some of the most necessary insights need the hardest work to accomplish.

○ 4. Write a book review on, or a letter to a friend about, or a personal account of, this book and its potential.

× 5. If you haven't had a celebration on your achievement in using this book now might be your last chance to plan it! What about a night off! Or a visit to your bookshop or library to get a book on leadership? Or might cream cakes for the family or flowers for your partner be better!

PREVIEW — POSTSCRIPT

WELCOME

If, like me, you often turn to the back of the book first then "Welcome", but you might make more sense of what follows if you read page 1 first. Maybe you will want to guess what is said before you do read there! If you have come here from page 1 then see how far you have managed to fathom my mind.

Why is he Writing This way?

I am trying to establish a relationship with you, the reader. I would like you to feel I am friendly and understanding, so that you feel comfortable with this book. Even if you don't use this book at least it makes the moments we have shared more significant. I hope you will sense that reading this book is intended to be a dynamic experience and not a passive one, for there are experiences woven into the text which can help you grow, as well as specific tasks at the end of each chapter. I also hope to lead you from where you are at this moment further on. I know I cannot order you. Anyway, I do not want to. I want to encourage and support you as you choose to develop or not. I want, even in my words, to express a Christian kind of leadership. So even if our journey together ends now I do appreciate the contact we have had.

Finally, I want to save your time. If we really can't work together perhaps it is best for both of us to find out now — and for you this is important, especially if you are wanting to understand about Christian leadership. So please don't let me put you off. Try one or more of the other good books available — the book list is on pages 176–186 and I have added some brief comments to help you choose the book(s) which will be most helpful for you. I know we have many disadvantages because we are not face to face. There is no body language, no personal way to keep our attention. It is difficult to affirm you and say "How about being friends?" I cannot respond to your needs directly because I have no feedback from you. So I am trying to overcome these difficulties, as I shall throughout the book.

Is he Succeeding?

Yes — then the next question is "How far is he succeeding?" Between us we could devise ways of measuring this, e.g. do you read the book? Do you use approach one, two or three (see page 6)? How far do you work with the book? How has your leadership, and understanding of leadership, developed? How will you assess this? More details on these points are to be found in the book.

No — probably you find my approach is annoying you. Please will you do two things?

1. Ask yourself why? Can you learn anything about yourself from your feelings?
2. Realizing my aims and problems can you do it better? I, too, want to learn and need your help. So please let me know your approach. Please send your comments addressed as follows:
   the Revd Dr D G Spriggs, c/o Bible Society, Stonehill Green, Westlea, Swindon, SN5 7DG

DRAFT LETTER TO PRAYER PARTNERS

Dear

I am about to start working through a book to help me develop my understanding of Christian leadership. I believe this book can help me be a better Christian leader in the Church of Jesus Christ and in my everyday life.

I realize that I will need God's help and personal support. I have prayed about this matter and believe that you could help me by being one of my ***prayer partners.***

I would hope to meet with you and another prayer partner once a week/fortnight for fourteen sessions whilst I work through this book. I would also share with you my needs and we would spend a few minutes in prayer together. (This need be no more than forty minutes altogether.) I would obviously be delighted to pray with, and for, you too. I would also like you to pray for me during the intervening times. In this way you would be playing a vital part in my growth.

Please can you let me know within a week. If I have not heard from you by then I will be in touch. If you want to ask me about anything please let me know.

Your Christian friend

APPENDIX A

GENERAL

Cyril Ashton, *Servant Spirit — Serving Church, Renewal in the local church* (Marshall Pickering, 1988).

This is a boldly written book. Its essential thesis is that if the Holy Spirit really penetrates the life of the people of God we will become a Church which serves the world in the name of God, because the essence of God's Spirit is service — the Spirit is a sending Spirit. In order to combat the tendency to internalize the Spirit's presence, visionary and enabling leadership is needed. The above indicates that the author is willing to face difficult issues openly and honestly. This is done in detail as well as on a wide canvas e.g. "women in leadership" (pp.64–70). There is an awareness of our Christian resources through Scripture and church history, as well as our Christian responsibility not only parochially, or even nationally, but world wide. There is real strength in the clarity and the challenge of this book.

Edward R Dayton and Ted W Engstom, *Strategy for Leadership, God's principles for Churches and Christian organizations* (Marc Europe, 1985).

Both authors write with considerable expertise within the secular management field; they have written several books seeking to apply these insights to the Christian one. The strength of this book is in helping the leader perceive the sociological factors operating in the Christian community and approaching these issues realistically.

It deals with issues such as goals, priorities, planning, evaluation. It is not so strong on the leader per se, nor people's needs in general. There are many practical insights to help any leader begin to move whose own approach is, or whose organization's attitudes are, stagnant.

General Synod Board of Education, *All are called, Towards a Theology of the Laity* (Church House Publishing, 1985).

This is a collection of nine essays seeking to understand the contribution of lay people in a changing secular and church scene. Although the essays are varied it does have some valuable insights and, throughout, indicates a commitment to utilizing and developing the ministry of every member of the Church, whilst recognizing that not all will contribute within the structures of the Church.

Eddie Gibbs, *I Believe in Church Growth* (Hodder and Stoughton, 1981).

This book is a must for all who want to understand the issues of church growth. It is written from a British perspective. Eddie Gibbs presented the initial rounds of church growth courses run by Bible Society. It includes much of the American insight. It is a large book of over 450 pages and is written lucidly. It moves from chapters on "God's People and the Nations" and "Gospel and Culture" to argue for the value of measuring what is going on in our Churches and how to do it, looks at groups and their contribution to growth, then to the wider issue of structures in Churches. The chapters on "Equipping and Mobilising" (which consider the issue of spiritual gifts) and "Leadership and Relationships" are the two most directly relevant to our subject. The final chapter on "Expectations and Planning" covers issues vital for any leader.

The book has four main virtues. It is written with contemporary knowledge of our Churches and the contexts in which we work. It is written out of a sensitive theological and biblical perspective. It is written with precision and clarity. It sets leadership in the wider context of growth. As Eddie says "There will be little in the way of sustained church growth without inspiring and facilitating leadership" (p.390).

Eddie Gibbs, *Body Building Exercises for the local church* (Falcon, 1979).

An early attempt to apply and present church growth understanding to the British scene. It has several good points. It is brief and it has some group session outlines. For those who are new to church growth or spiritual gift issues it remains a useful starting place.

Leadership

Anton Baumohl, *Grow Your Own Leaders, A practical guide to training in the local church* (Scripture Union, 1987).

This book believes that training is the basis for providing the Church with leaders. "Training for service is an integral part of being a Christian disciple" (p.24). Training is defined as "those activities that help equip people to carry out a particular task or take on some specific responsibility" (p.33). It makes extensive use of case studies and to this extent is rooted in practicalities.

It presents three models of training — apprenticeship, distance, and training course — and looks at the skills of the trainer and resources for training, and encourages churches to develop a training strategy. It is a valuable resource tool for those who want to develop and equip the members of the Church. There is perhaps not so much here about leaders.

Paul Beasley-Murray, *Dynamic Leadership, Making it Work for You and Your Church. Rising above the chaos of the one-man band* (Marc, 1990).

This is written by a man who likes to lead and to make things happen. He writes with a lively style which flows from a vigorous mind. Four out of the ten chapters are about teams. Following a look at biblical leadership, which focuses on Jesus, there are chapters on defining and achieving the task, sections on teams, a look at the qualities a leader needs and finally an encouragement to maintain as primary our relationship with God. It is written for workers in the church context and the Baptist church specifically. It understands such leadership as primarily pastoral leadership.

John Eddison, *Understanding Leadership* (Scripture Union, 1974).

This book is written in response to the popular cry "Where have all the leaders gone?" It recognizes that charismatic leaders such as Churchill, Temple, and Kennedy appear rarely and that there are many "ordinary, run of the mill leaders's today, as leadership is more widely spread. Leadership is also difficult today.

The book is a study of leadership as it was exercised by ten of the most outstanding people in the Bible — Joseph, Moses, Joshua, Samson, Samuel, David, Daniel, John, Simon Peter, Paul. It is easy to read and has perceptive comments. At the end of each chapter are some "Discussion points" but they are more to do with the biblical character than personal growth. Its weaknesses are its strengths. First, it can only be superficial because it covers ten people (is the balance right, and can Christians afford to leave out Jesus?). Secondly, most of us are not the most outstanding, and therefore distanced from the chosen ten, even if attention is given to their weaknesses as well as their strengths.

John Finney, *Understanding Leadership* (Daybreak, 1989).

John Finney writes with an Anglican background and out of a fascination with current management theory. To this he brings an understanding of a distinctively Christian view of leadership and a sensitivity to the impact of renewal on congregations. His interest in management theory is reflected in the clarity of presentation, the insights he integrates and the diagrammatic presentations which are sprinkled through the book.

It is a mentally more demanding book than many of the contemporary books on Christian leadership (hence the "Understanding" in the title is appropriate). However the person of the leader is not neglected for structural concerns. There are useful chapters on the strains and joys of leadership. Also valuable is the chapter on change. This book is to be highly recommended to those who want to understand leadership issues more thoroughly. Some will find its biblical basis thinner than they would wish. First impressions are not always right!

Philip Greenslade, *Leadership, Patterns for Biblical Leadership Today* (Marshalls Paperbacks, 1984).

Although written from within the charismatic house church movement by someone who has moved from main line Baptist tradition, this book is a must for anyone wanting to understand the challenges and possibilities of leadership within the Christian Church today, whichever branch they belong to.

It has four main sections:

Why Leadership?
Looking At Leadership
Follow My Leader
Leadership Today

Sections 2 and 3 are full of biblical insight, section 3 drawing heavily on the model of leadership Jesus provided. The final section looks at the application of biblical kinds of leaders to contemporary church life dealing with apostles, prophets, preachers, equippers, troubleshooters, overseers, and envisioners — although these are not his titles.

Philip King, *Leadership Explosion, Maximising Leadership Potential in the Church* (Hodder and Stoughton, 1987).

Starting from the sociologist's perspective on leadership styles, Philip King moves in Chapter 2 to Asia, Africa, South America, and the USA, thus he brings to bear his own experience of these areas. This is more technical and less biblical than many of the popular books on Christian leadership that are available. Chapter 3 seeks to gain principles from the Bible about leadership which are then worked out in the rest of the book. Issues such as shared leadership, renewing structures, the purpose of our leadership, developing other people's leadership are dealt with. This book is a good mix of management theory, personal experience in a worldwide context, and contemporary spirituality. Perhaps the flavour of it is best caught in a quotation. "'If I hadn't been trained in the RAF on how to manage a unit', commented a Midland vicar, 'renewal wouldn't have happened in this parish in the way it has'". This book also represents a strongly Anglican ethos!

Andrew T Le Peau, *Paths of Leadership* (IVP, 1985).

This book sets out "to present a Christian view of leadership". Whilst recognizing the value of a practical approach the author chooses a "pastoral rather than managerial" emphasis, underlining the vital contribution of character to leadership. He regards leadership as a function, not a position, hence he deals with various functions — serving, following, facilitating, teaching, modelling, envisioning.

Whilst dealing with functions the book is full of humans — stories, quotations, biographical references. It is a lively, easy to read book, well sprinkled with biblical references, but rarely the quotation of scriptures. The heart cry of the book is "everyone leads", by which the author means "everyone, at one time or another, fulfils a leadership role" so we need to learn to lead together.

Calvin Miller, *Leadership, An influencer discussion guide* (Navpress, 1987).

This book uses the life of David, as portrayed in Scripture, to illuminate Christian awareness of, and response to, leadership issues. Calvin Miller has the business as well as the Christian spheres in view. Each of the thirteen sections begins with a few quotations, then mentions a scripture passage. The main section is an introduction to the theme, using mainly contemporary insights, with a movement back to the biblical passage. This is then explored through questions directed to the passage. The thirteen sections include the perception and the friends of the leader, vision, decision, motivating, delegation, coping with difficult people, adjustments in style. So thematically it is relevant to most of the issue dealt with in this book. I particularly like Chapter 9 on "Leadership and the Abuse of Power".

John Perry, *Effective Christian Leadership* (Hodder, 1987).

This brief book of 160 pages covers many features of Christian leadership. Its strength is therefore that it gives a good balance and introduction. Its inevitable weakness is that it cannot deal in detail with any aspect of leadership. The biblical features of leadership, the person the leader needs to be, the styles of leadership and the functions of leading — they are all there, along with time management, home life, cost, and accountability. Add to this a tendency to wander from the theme (how much of Chapter 9 "Reaching Men" is really about leadership?). Nevertheless there is much to interest and enlighten. For me the best chapter is "Listening to Others" and the favourite quotation "Effective leadership is about enabling Christians to be what they are — eagles not chickens" — although to understand this you will need to read *A story from Africa* which precedes it.

C Peter Wagner, *Leading Your Church to Growth* (Marc, 1984).

This book could be considered the exposition of Eddie Gibbs's text "There will be little in the way of sustained church growth without inspiring and facilitating leadership". It focuses on the vital contribution of the pastor to church growth (or not). Thus it is a churchy book. It is written easily, with anecdotes, but also with the analytical background of the Fuller Church Growth School. Throughout, we are aware of the American context, but there is much insight and much to challenge us. Whilst its focus is the significance of leadership, it recognizes that leadership is always in tandem with the congregation. Particularly relevant are chapter 2, "Church Growth Is Not Cheap — the Pastor's and People's Price for Growth"; chapter 3, "Church Growth Pastor = Leader + Equipper"; and chapter 7, "Keeping Growth on Course".

Specific Issues

Arnold Bittlinger, *Gifts and Graces, A Commentary on 1 Corinthians 12—14,* (Hodder and Stoughton, 1967).

This is a very brief, but useful, biblically based introduction to the subject of spiritual gifts. It comes from the earlier days of the charismatic renewal and is developed from lectures delivered at an ecumenical conference.

Arnold Bittlinger, *Gifts and Ministries* (Hodder and Stoughton, 1974).

This book originated as separate booklets and perhaps suffers some discontinuities. Nevertheless it is valuable. Bittlinger starts from the premise that Christian ministry functions as a form of stewardship. He believes that "gifts" and "office" should supplement each other. Beginning with the various offices, first in the local congregation (bishop, deacons) then for the whole church (apostle, prophets, evangelist, shepherd, teacher) he examines the conditions and qualities required in the New Testament (and occasionally patristically), working towards the gifts appropriate for each ministry. His final chapter "Gifts and Ministries" is an exposition of the parable of the pounds (Luke 19.11–27).

David Cormack, *Seconds Away, Fifteen rounds in the fight for effective use of time,* (Marc Europe, 1986).

This book is extremely hard work. Not because it is long (it is just over 150 pages of text) nor because it is written imprecisely, nor because it deals with an obscure subject. It is hard work because, from the start, it demands application and change if it is to be of any value. It is written, quite appropriately in the light of my comments above, on the analogy of a fifteen round boxing context. Why? "Boxing involves skill, determination and effort. Changing the way you live will not be easy". The change envisaged is not directly a moral or religious change, it is about maximizing the use of our time. It does recognize people have very varied capacities. It helps us work out what we want to achieve and how we can achieve it. It helps us find resources and cope with our opponents.

It is a powerful and a positive book when taken seriously. Two warnings for the casual reader. "Benefits you will have already, (through reading the book) but do not settle for second best. Commit yourself to the three year discipline" (p.171). "Never lose sight of the fact that you are the greatest enemy in your fight for life — no one wastes your time as much as you do!" (p.177). Just occasionally I sense the drive of the book becomes too selfish to be fully Christian. Pin a boxer on the ropes!?

David Cormack, *Team Spirit, People working with people,* (Marc Europe, 1987).

This book is not written for churches. By this I mean it is not written up for, and applied to, church situations. Yet it is essential reading for all involved in leading churches or other Christian organizations. It has five main sections:

Committing yourself to the process (of building teams)
Acquiring the skills
Applying the skills
Evaluating your performance
Building on your experience

It is written from the conviction "The benefits that come from being part of a strong group cannot be over-estimated". It is also written out of the experience of one who has worked hard and successfully in industry and with Christians. Thus the writer knows the problems as well as the potential. This book has insight, practical help, humour, encouragement, and enthusiasm. A must for anyone who wants to work successfully with groups of people for God. This book is also written out of the conviction that most of the principles for teams can be found in Scripture. It is part and parcel of the fundamentally Christian perspective that more attention is given to the people in the team than to the tasks they are to accomplish. "If the leader can enhance the self regard of the members… then the team will work well" (p.144).

Joanne Feldmeth, *Leader's Guide for C Peter Wagner's Your Spiritual Gifts* (Regal Books, 1984).

This thirteen session guide is thoroughly American. It envisages the American all age Sunday school context and the style of presentation and content are clearly American. This is not to denigrate the book. I would commend it as a basis for those who want to develop people's gifts in a church context. But it is to recognize that it needs a lot of work on it before it will be thoroughly acceptable to a British readership.

G A Getz, *The Measure of a Man,* Regal, 1974.
G A Getz, *The Measure of a Woman,* Regal, 1974.

The objectives of both books are similar — to enable people to become more mature Christian people. They are more pertinent to Christian leadership than might at first appear because the basis for them is largely the Pauline passages about leaders in the Church (1 Timothy 3; Titus 1). Both books are helpful to either men or women just because they are about Christian maturity. On the basis of biblical insight which is clearly explained, each chapter proceeds to a personal project to help the reader become what they have read about. In the words of the author:

> *Each chapter in this book is self-contained, presenting a biblical mark or characteristic of Christian maturity... At the end of each chapter there are practical steps to assist you in developing this particular quality in your life (*Woman *p.9 cf.* Man *p.10)*

They are part of a larger series which includes *The Measure of a Marriage/Family/Church.*

Joyce Huggett, *Conflict Friend or Foe?* (Kingsway, 1984).

This book is written very much with the domestic situation in mind. Nevertheless it provides many insights into the way conflicts develop and some ways in which they can be resolved. Because it is written with sensitivity and seeks to apply scriptual principles, it has a contribution to make for leaders wishing to understand how conflicts arise within groups, particularly in church groups which in some respects are more like a family group than a business situation. There is, however, one chapter devoted to "Friction in the Fellowship" which has particular relevance.

Gordon Macdonald, *Restoring Your Spiritual Passion* (Highland Books, 1986).

The warm, sensitive, personal style of the author helps the British reader cope with the americanisms and the reflection of American culture. The great value of this book is that it helps us recognize the consequences of stress and the dark side of our souls, and face them and provides solutions. I found the analysis of the effects of different kinds of people on us, and the commendation of special friends who restore us, very helpful. They come in various guises, the sponsor, the affirmer, the rebuker, the intercessor, the partner, the pastor. Every leader needs help to keep his spiritual passion glowing. This book at least provides clues.

David Pytches, *Come, Holy Spirit. Learning how to minister in power* (Hodder and Stoughton, 1985).

Although the focus of this book is the healing ministry of the Church, its value for us lies in its descriptive definitions and biblical statements concerning certain spiritual gifts i.e. tongues, interpretation, prophecy, discernment, words of wisdom and knowledge, faith, miraculous powers, healing. These accounts should be read in conjunction with C P Wagner's.

Myron Rush, *Burnout, Practical help for lives under pressure* (Victor Books, 1989).

This book is written to help people, and to help others help those, who are suffering from burnout, or stress symptoms. It is written by an American and has a very American feel to it. It is full of personal anecdotes, which will help some grasp the points. It analyzes the nature of burnout and practical remedies for it. It encourages us to live within our God-given resources and work for our God-given priorities. It also helps us gain from the experience of burnout. Even here "God is at work for good with those who love him..." Thus it is written sympathetically and positively.

Charles Sibthorpe, *A Man Under Authority, Qualities of Christian leadership* (Kingsway, 1984).

This book, which is quite openly from the charismatic side of the church (how many sides does the church have? Is it a triangle, a hexagon?), has much to say to all sides and to both sexes. "The title of this book is not intended to confine its readership to men only!... This book is for all who are called to leadership... The basic principle is that leaders lead by example" (p.19).

Hence, whilst the subtitle refers to leadership the claim is made, and the book written, from the belief that "God is more interested in the worker than the work" (p.194). The book is in two main parts:

1. The quality of a leader's life, dealing with the leader's relationship with God, and what flows from it.
2. The principles of a leader's work, including the need for the gospel, the Spirit, the word, prayer, faith, humility, compassion, and courage. It is an engaging book, although somewhat dictatorial in tone. It is full of scriptual comment and personal testimony. It is written out of the author's involvement in helping leaders move forward, through the leaders' weeks held at the Hyde.

C Peter Wagner, *Your Spiritual Gifts Can Help Your Church Grow, How to find your gift and use it* (Marc Europe, 1985).

Following an autobiographical introduction the author introduces us to the issue of spiritual gifts and some of the controversial issues. The readers are then introduced to specific spiritual gifts. These are grouped around roles in the church, the pastor, the evangelist, the missionary gift (this enables Wagner to present fourteen gifts). The final ten are "the rest of the body". Wagner is not essentially a theoretician. He wants people to discover their gifts and get on and use them. He wants to help people find their gifts because if we fulfil roles for which we are not suited we lose effectiveness. He is concerned to challenge churches and their teachers to enable people's gifts to be employed. "Few things can be more frustrating than discovering a spiritual gift and not being able to use it in the church" (p.248). Wagner's analysis of the spiritual gifts needs to be balanced with that of David Pytches in *Come, Holy Spirit.* Most of Wagner's insights are assimilated in Eddie Gibbs, *I Believe In Church Growth.*

APPENDIX B

Here is a brief introduction to ten biographies of Christian leaders. If none of these appeals then how can we proceed? In the last five years over 9,000 biographies have been published in Britain. Although most of these are not specifically on Christian leaders they will nearly all give some insight for our subject. A visit to the local library will give us some idea of what is available. Alternatively, we can begin with books which give a brief resume of a number of people's lives. Then, having found a subject which interests us, we can ask the library to order a book about them. William Purcell has written three books which help in this respect:

Ten Outstanding Social Reformers, (Mowbray, 1987)
Ten Outstanding Witnesses for God, (Mowbray, 1987)
Ten Outstanding Spiritual Leaders, (Mowbray, 1987)

If we know the person whose life we want to follow but not the book we want to read, or if we become fascinated by the leader's life and want to read several books about them, then larger libraries can provide information about all the books available on a person. We need to ask if they have an "On line search facility for British books in print". A charge is normally made for this service.

Dorothy Clarke Wilson, *Ten Fingers for God* (Hodder & Stoughton, 1966).

This is the story of Paul Brand born in 1914 who developed pioneering surgical techniques to restore movement to the limbs of people whose hands and feet had been damaged through the loss of feelings caused by leprosy. He was born of medical missionary parents. He shared their love for India, its needy people and God. This is not only the story of a pioneering surgeon, it is also about a true leader's struggles with prejudices and bureaucracy. It is the story of building a community and of how a leader copes with crises. It is the story of vision and co-operation and of how "an impulse generated by a little team of workers in Vellore had helped to spark a chain reaction of human concern which was stimulating a fresh appraisal of the problem on all continents" (p.245).

A similar theme is covered by Phyliss Thompson's *Mister Leprosy* (Hodder & Stoughton).

Richard Collier, *The General Next to God* (Fontana, 1965).

This is subtitles "The story of William Booth and the Salvation

Army". However, as 90% of the book deals with the period of William Booth it can still be considered a biography. Although written anecdotally it gives a clear impression of this amazing leader's strengths and weaknesses. Through his life's development we glimpse the history of his day and indeed see the world as the work of the Salvation Army expands. Although Booth is seen as something of an autocratic general, we are also given the impression that no one can accomplish such amazing things without the support of many other leaders.

Desmond Doig, *Mother Teresa: Her People and Her Work* (Collins Fount Paperbacks, 1978).
Angelo Devananda, *Mother Teresa: Contemplative at the Heart of the World* (Fount Paperbacks, 1986).

These two books taken together give valuable insight into the leadership qualities of one of the most famous women of our day. Mother Teresa is well known for her commitment to care for the world's poor and destitute. Starting in Calcutta, her mission has now established work in several continents. The first book tells a little of Mother Teresa's life (although she is most reticent), and more about her work. Different perspectives are given as we learn of Mother Teresa's life through the eyes of those who know her and work with her. The second deals more with her own thoughts and spiritually and gives us a clue as to how this little lady can be so powerful for God.

John Pollock, *Billy Graham* (Hodder and Stoughton, 1967).

An interestingly written account of one of the world's greatest evangelists. It is based on careful research but is presented in a light, personal and fast moving style. A clear picture of the person in the context of his times is given. Some attempt to assess the impact of his work is also made. It is, of course, limited by the fact that Graham has "gone on" for another 25 years.

John Pollock has written several other biographies including Whitfield, Shaftesbury, Wilberforce, Hudson Taylor and Moody.

John G Clancy *Apostle For Our Time: Pope Paul VI* (Collins, 1963).

In this book we are given a clear picture of the development of a frail baby boy into a strong vigorous leader of the Catholic Church. But his story is more than one of personal development. It is development in the context of a changing backcloth of different societies and of Catholic history. Yet such backcloths are on the whole necessary. Nevertheless we gain a clear picture of the man. We are shown the strengths of an unusual blend of character: sensitivity, intelligence, passion for truth and justice — and of roles: pastor, diplomat, communicator. We see a man at home in the religious world of the Vatican and the secular world of the twentieth century. As one said of him "What a man! What a heart! He was the easiest man in the world to talk to, and he made me feel very good" (pp. 52-53).

Shirley Du Boulay, *Tutu: Voice of the Voiceless* (Hodder and Stoughton, 1988).

This skilfully planned and clearly written book succeeds in portraying a "larger than life" twentieth century Christian leader. "A profoundly spiritual man... widely travelled, witty and courteous, with a quick silver mind and a disarming honesty" (p. 181). Insight into politics and theology are here in plenty. But also into the development of a richly Christian man who has had, even with the odds so heavily stacked against him, an amazing impact on his country and the western world. In addition to the accolades quoted above, others like "humble, courageous, passionate, diplomatic, and man of peace" come readily to mind.

Here is a leader who exemplifies so much, not least how to cope with pressure!

Jackie Pullinger with Andrew Quicke, *Chasing the Dragon* (Hodder and Stoughton, 1980).

This is a fast moving autobiographical account of the activities of a young music teacher in the dark "Walled City" of Hong Kong. With a middle class upbringing Jackie, frustrated by attempts to discover God's will theoretically, takes the advice of a minister to go on the longest boat journey she can. Eventually, relying only on God, she arrives in Hong Kong and becomes involved in ministry to drug addicts, prostitutes and crime gangs. The only difficulty with this book, from our point of view, is discerning how Jackie leads. Clearly she does not work alone! Yet there are illuminating glimpses — watch out for them carefully!

Edwin Robertson, *The Shame and the Sacrifice* (Hodder and Stoughton, 1987).

This is a more difficult book from our point of view for three reasons. First it is a more academic biography then most, containing many lengthy quotations, and is more historically critical. Secondly, it tells the story of the complex personality of Dietrich Bonhoeffer, the German pastor and theologian whose thoughts, often embryonic and sometimes perplexingly paradoxical, have had such a profound influence on modern western theology. Thirdly, it tells of a leader who breaks the rules for he did not, during the formative time of his life, have a group of followers.

Nevertheless there is much insight here for any Christian leader. A book and a person well worth the effort to discover.

Norman Anderson, *An Adopted Son* (IVP, 1985).

This is an autobiography, and a very personal one at that. The author intended it to be a book about God "bringing many sons to glory", illustrated from his own experience, but such a book proved too difficult. The author is a well known evangelical Anglican. The backcloth to part of his life is the Middle East, including the years of the Second World War. Essentially an academic legal scholar the book shows a wide range of insights into a leader's role, both within the church and in society. Although at times the personal details clog the scene from our point of view they also remind us that leaders have to cope with their own bodies, and the ups and downs of family life too.

Edited Edward England, *David Watson: a portrait by his friends* (Highland Books, 1985).

The subject of this book is the evangelical, charismatic Anglican leader who became well known for two very different reasons. First, the amazing transformation of a dying church in York, and then his own dying, of cancer. This book is unusual in two respects. First, it was written soon after, and probably because of the impact of his death. Whilst there are some dangers with this, there are also some values, not least that they remind us that every leaders and everyone of us has, unavoidably, a limited life span. The second unusual feature is that twelve different people comment on twelve aspects of David's life and ministry e.g. living in community, the author, his ministry in the church, his involvement with the theatre company "Riding Lights".

For those who want to know David Watson from the inside he has written two autobiographical accounts: *You are my God* (Hodder and Stoughton, 1983) and *Fear No Evil* (Hodder and Stoughton, 1984).

APPENDIX C

Further Help

Administry

0727 56370	Offers training in creative administration
69 Sandridge Road	
St Albans	
Herts AL1 4AG	

Association for Promoting Retreats

071 493 3534	Information and training for retreats
Liddon House	
24 South Audley Street	
London W1Y 5DL	

Bible Society

0793 513713	Literature and training courses to develop gifts and ministries, and leadership
Stonehill Green	
Swindon	
Wilts SN5 7DG	

British Church Growth Ass.

071 793 0264	Share insight and experience of church growth
St Mark's Chambers	
Kennington Road	
London SE11 4PW	

Evangelical Alliance

071 582 0228	Co-ordination of information and equipping for evangelical churches and organizations
186 Kennington Park Road	
London SE11 4BT	

Marc Europe

081 460 3999	Materials and training for Christian leadership
Cosmos House	
6 Homesdale Road	
Bromley	
Kent BR2	

National Christian Education Council

073 782 2411	Training and materials for
Robert Denholm House	development of Christian education
Nutfield	
Redhill	
Surrey RH1 4HW	

Scripture Union

0272 771131	Provides literature and training
9 Clothier Road	for Christian education
Bristol	
Avon BS4 5RL	

Some training resources can be found in A Baumohl, *Grow Your Own Leaders* (Scripture Union, 1987), pp.175–187.

Many more resources can be found in *UK Christian Handbook* (Marc Europe).